Imagining the Church

Keeping Faith in a Fragmented World

— TIM GIBSON —

Sacristy Press

Sacristy Press
PO Box 612, Durham, DH1 9HT

www.sacristy.co.uk

First published in 2021 by Sacristy Press, Durham

Copyright © Tim Gibson 2021
The moral rights of the author have been asserted.

All rights reserved, no part of this publication may be reproduced or transmitted in any form or by any means, electronic, mechanical photocopying, documentary, film or in any other format without prior written permission of the publisher.

Scripture quotations, unless otherwise stated, are from the New Revised Standard Version Bible: Anglicized Edition, copyright © 1989, 1995 National Council of the Churches of Christ in the United States of America. Used by permission. All rights reserved worldwide.

Every reasonable effort has been made to trace the copyright holders of material reproduced in this book, but if any have been inadvertently overlooked the publisher would be glad to hear from them.

Sacristy Limited, registered in England & Wales, number 7565667

British Library Cataloguing-in-Publication Data
A catalogue record for the book is available from the British Library

ISBN 978-1-78959-182-8

Contents

Preface iv
Acknowledgments viii
Introduction 1

Chapter 1. Coming home 9
Chapter 2. Time and eternity .23
Chapter 3. Parish and particularity 36
Chapter 4. Somewhere and anywhere 51
Chapter 5. Though we are many 63
Chapter 6. Growth and glory .80
Chapter 7. Marking time 94
Chapter 8. Keeping and sharing 107
Coda. The parish in lockdown 120

Notes 125

Preface

Here is an imagining of the church, an attempt to reflect on its essence as I have perceived it in a number of contexts, over a number of years. In describing my experiences, I seek to unlock the perceptions of my readers, to turn the cogs of their imaginings. In that, I hope, will be found something of the *real* essence of our church, always perceived fleetingly, imprecisely, in fragments that dance before our eyes and soon pass into the uncertainties of the future.

Each chapter in this short book is one such fragment, offered in humility in the hope of connecting with other fragments, some similar and many more different. If there are common themes, it is because that's how imagination works: we return to the same stories, are inspired by the same images, even as we give them new expression. Like the motifs and phrases that recur in a symphony, we circle around the same ideas, each time expressing them differently, each time finding some fresh meaning in them. But all the time we are aware that the whole is more than these parts, always capable of exceeding itself even as we acknowledge its incompleteness.

That, I think, is the force of imagination. It is an imprecise act, a habit that we form at the earliest age and then spend our lives unlearning. But we cannot escape our disposition towards flights of fancy, even if we spend a lot of time denying it. The church's life and worship serve as daily reminders of that: this is what it is to cast your eyes beyond the world as you observe it and imagine a different version of it. Or so it seems to me.

And so I have noted my imaginings, not least to see how they intersect, to stand back from them and see what patterns emerge. That is all I have done: narrate my imaginings, sometimes by reference to the sources that have shaped them, or helped me to make fleeting sense of them, and more often by reference to the experience itself, of being present in a church in a given time and place, and imagining what it is to stand there before God, meekly asking what is required of me. They are partial, fragmentary and often poorly worked out—not scholarly at all. But what is important is not their substance, still less that they are *my* imaginings. What matters is that they establish a pattern for thinking about the church that rescues us from empirical surveys and partisan polemic. They are the records of an Anglican priest and writer, struggling to make sense of the world but finding the struggle itself somehow helpful, somehow meaningful. I hope you find them to be that way, too.

Some broad themes

For those in search of order, the following represents a broad set of principles by reference to which the discourse is loosely arranged, with plenty of circling back to where I have come from and ahead to where I may be going: place and identity (Chapter 1); time and eternity (Chapter 2); parish and particularity (Chapter 3); the local and the national (Chapter 4); unity and diversity (Chapter 5); growth and glory (Chapter 6); seasonal worship (Chapter 7); and ministry and mission (Chapter 8). A short coda begins to explore the experience of moving church services online during the 2020–1 COVID-19 pandemic.

If there is an overarching motif, it is this: that the Church of England *matters*, that it has an enduring place in the imaginations of many in contemporary society and that we should keep faith with it, even if we sometimes feel beleaguered, irrelevant, taken for granted or forgotten. It is our privilege as the nation's church to be present everywhere but rarely noticed. Just keep the faith. That's all we're called to do.

I explore my themes in the manner of a personal essay. In keeping with that form, I've kept referencing light—including footnotes only when I think the reader may be interested to follow up a source for further reading. I hope these references don't interfere with the flow of the text. Like many works of this ilk, you could ignore them and not lose anything from the thrust of the discussion, though you would miss exposure to a rich vein of literature of far higher quality than the book you hold in your hands.

Tim Gibson
Mothering Sunday, 2021

Acknowledgments

It is impossible to thank all the people who have shaped the experiences that this book recounts, but I would draw attention to a few faithful friends who have guided, encouraged and supported me along the way.

I feel lucky to work in a uniquely creative environment at the University of the West of England and note particular gratitude to James Murphy and Harriet Castor Jeffery for their leadership, humour and companionship.

Mark Charlton, a friend who became a colleague, has been a wonderful sounding board and read a whole draft of this volume, offering the perspective of a non-churchgoer with grace and elegance. I greatly value his insights and friendship and remain a huge admirer of his writing.

Students and colleagues from the South West Ministry Training Course, Sarum College, the Diocese of Bath and Wells, and the Bright Field Community will be familiar with much of what follows. I am especially grateful to all of them, past and present, for their companionship and enthusiasm for the task of theological formation. Their unquenchable desire to participate in God's mission with faithfulness and joy is a daily inspiration to me.

Thanks to a brace of archdeacons—Simon Hill and Catherine Sourbut Groves—for reading and commenting on various drafts of this project and especially for their encouragement to publish. Thanks, too, to my friend and former colleague Kathy O'Loughlin, who read and faithfully commented on a near-final draft of this book and whose detailed feedback was enlightening, encouraging and to the clear betterment of the manuscript. Of course, any errors or shortcomings are resolutely my own.

To my companions in the Isle Valley Benefice. Over thirteen years together, they have nurtured my vocation and put up with my failings with huge grace and no small amount of humour. I especially thank Andrew Tatham and Phil Denison, who, as successive incumbents of the benefice, have proved such helpful and wise colleagues. I also thank Greg Hoare and Philip Albrow, both valued friends who have taught me a great deal.

Special thanks to my publisher and editor, Natalie Watson, whose belief in and intuitive understanding of this project have been crucial to its arrival in the world. I also note my gratitude for the efforts of Sarah Parkinson, who copy-edited the manuscript with a deft touch.

To my family—especially Mum and Dad, Philip and Melanie, Richard and Sarah, and all my nephews and nieces—thank you for being a source of strength, hope and glory in a fallen world.

Thanks, too, to Ads Miller, a lifelong friend who gave me my first copy of *Three Mile Man*, knowing by instinct that it would become a favourite. It is a joy to know so deeply and to be so deeply known.

And to Sarah, Monty and Florence—the loves of my life. You are my heart, still beating. Thank you.

This book is dedicated to Father David Moss, who has done more than anyone to shape my imagining of the Church of England and my understanding of what it means to be a priest within it. My work will never be worthy of your intellect, but I hope you can see the echoes of our conversations in these pages. Like so many priests who have been formed by your example, I am grateful for your care, compassion and sheer humanity.

Introduction

St Peter's, Ilton

I can't get Ralph Vaughan Williams out of my head. *The Lark Ascending* echoes around my imagination, soundtracking the scene before me. Like the music, it is almost laughably bucolic, like something from a picture postcard or a Sunday evening television drama. Clambering from the car, parked up beside a well-clipped village green, I face a quaint country pub with whitewashed walls and a pink tiled roof. Thatched cottages stand on either side, some with willows tumbling in their front gardens and others with rose-framed front porches. If I listen carefully, I can hear the strains of a cricket match coming to an end on the pitch beside the village hall, the celebratory shouts of the victorious team drifting on the warm evening breeze. I half expect Miss Marple to appear on a pushbike, brow furrowed as she ponders some gruesome murder or other. It's all I can do not to walk into the pub and order a pint of warm bitter to sip while completing my *Sunday Times* crossword.

But it's an urge I resist because the bell for evensong is tolling and I must hasten to church. Even in these days of greater lay involvement, the service is unlikely to proceed until the local cleric arrives, cassock on and raring to go. So I straighten my dog collar, rub my shoes against the back of my trousers in an effort to clear the grime picked up in the graveyard at yesterday's burial of ashes, and head for the vestry.

Given the idealized village I've been describing, you might expect me to find a church packed with parishioners. This particular village—the largest of the eight in which I serve—has a population of nearly one thousand souls. Even if only five per cent attend the service, I should expect a congregation of around fifty. Miss Marple would be unimpressed by any fewer.

But my congregation numbers just four people plus a dog. You know you're on sticky ground when you count the dogs. These are faithful people, whom I have grown to love dearly. When I see their faces crease into warm smiles of greeting, I am overcome by their sheer faithfulness, their unwillingness to roll over and concede defeat to the forces of secularism. For them, this disciplined witness, this weekly attendance in a cold church with poor light and heating and an organ that squeaks in all the wrong places, is the ultimate sign of love. It is a sign of their fervent belief that God relishes their company, is present in their worship, giving them a glimpse of heaven and the saints in glory. Where two or three are gathered, they believe, there he shall be.

And they are right. We *do* join the saints in heaven as we sing our hymns and tread our way uncertainly through ancient psalms and canticles. Even with our weak voices and frail bodies, we are made whole, bound up in glory. Transcended even as we gather in our human weakness, beleaguered but not beaten, disappointed but not despairing.

Of course we would like to be joined by more of our neighbours. We believe we are called to make disciples of all nations, not to live in a holy huddle, doors closed to the waiting world. But, frankly, we just don't have the energy to compete with the draw of Sunday evening cricket, *Antiques Roadshow* and *Countryfile* on TV. We're tired. The congregation is elderly. The church is poor. Surely, for now, it's enough to cup our hands around the flame and keep it burning in the darkness. Others will come along one day to set the world alight again.

When Agatha Christie invented Miss Marple, the village church was something to be relied upon, much like her sensible tweeds. Taken for granted, really. Along with the rose-framed cottages and village cricket, warm beer and broadsheet crosswords, it was a part of the very fabric of rural communities. The church was just *there*, doing its thing. And even if attendance fluctuated, even if agnosticism and atheism began to eat into the public consciousness, the church still had a role. It held the transcendent in the midst of the earthly, even for those who no longer believed in the existence of anything beyond this world. It curated and marshalled the big moments in life: festivals and feasts, births, deaths and marriages. It was a steady presence in the community, and, at some deep level, it could rely on the people to support it, respect it, appreciate its worth. There was a social contract between church and society: we're here for one another, even if we're sometimes out of step.

Nowadays, that contract has been disrupted. It's easy to point the finger at Richard Dawkins and others like him, to blame the rise of militant atheism, but that's not fair. Even the briefest of surveys of the Victorian church (I heartily recommend Owen Chadwick's classic two-volume history of the era if you share my interest[1]) reveals that non-belief is by no means a phenomenon of the late twentieth century. People have been not believing in God for generations, yet the decline in churchgoing is more recent. If there's a difference between now and then, it's that people are more willing to admit to their doubts now.

Like many Anglicans, I've never regarded belief as a reliable predictor of church attendance. I don't buy that the decline in churchgoing has been shaped by the rise in atheism. As it happens, I don't fundamentally believe that people *have* stopped believing in God. They've just lost the language in which to articulate the belief they do have. Atheism hasn't won. In fact, it's retreating, as even Richard Dawkins seems tacitly to acknowledge in his more recent writings.[2]

So this church isn't nearly empty because people no longer believe in what we're offering, in what we represent. It's my contention that they still want to see the candle burning, still want to see its flickering light and, just occasionally, to gather around the gentle warmth of its flame. But most of the time, they're happy to see the light from the outside reflected in stained-glass windows, to smell the warm wax when popping into church on a quiet Monday to light a votive candle in a moment of peaceful contemplation. So long as some of us keep the flame burning week by week, holding it on behalf of the whole community, everyone is reassured, everyone is happy.

Imagining the parish church

Now, then, is a moment to explore this church that I adore, represented as it is by the hundreds of parish churches up and down the country that are loved and valued but rarely attended for Sunday worship. I want to tease out my instinct for a church that is not yet abandoned, not yet without hope: to discover what it is that characterizes this church in the twenty-first century. What's it all about? What does it stand for? And, more fundamentally, how is it shaped by, and how does it shape, the imaginations of the people who live beside it and occasionally go inside? For that, it seems to me, is the fundamental feature of our church: it works on and in our imaginations, as an idea that is more than idea, always exceeding itself and always shaping our perceptions of the world.

And so to my task. A task that encompasses individual, particular churches just like the one where I kneel for evensong with these four faithful disciples (not forgetting the dog). But it also considers the presentation of the church in public imagination, in fiction and on television, contributing as these portrayals do to the picture we hold of the church in our hearts and minds.

I am confident in what I shall discover: a church that gestures towards a God who is very much alive and well, who longs for us to know him and to make him fully known. I am not persuaded that religion is a thing of the past, best confined to the world of Agatha Christie, warm beer and village cricket. As the Psalmist likes to remind us, God doesn't go away, even if we stop noticing him for a while. God remains faithful and true, calling us into his life and promising to make us whole again. So he continues to exercise a pull on our imaginations, individually and corporately. And the local, parish, church—bearing witness to Christ in the midst of our communities—mediates that pull and helps us make fleeting sense of it.

Which is why I feel so moved by these faithful people gathered in a country church for a summer evensong. They truly are Christ, present to the world: faithful as he is faithful, loving as he is loving, patient as he is patient, kind as he is kind. These people are the salt of the earth, flavouring the stew: the yeast leavening the loaf. They are the living embodiment of what Michael Ramsey memorably described as the "fragment of the fragment"—made whole by their brokenness, given strength not in spite of their frailty but because of it. Of this church, he wrote: "Its credentials are its incompleteness, with the tension and the travail in its soul. It is clumsy and untidy, it baffles neatness and logic. For it is sent not to commend itself as the 'best type of

Christianity', but by its very brokenness to point to the universal Church."[3]

This is the church I want to learn more about, to dwell with and uncover. This is the church that I love, that somehow glimpses the future even while it seems caught up in the past: a fragmentary, broken church; a place of vulnerability, in which the frail gather and know that they are cherished. And, as Ramsey suggests, discovering it is unlikely to permit neat thinking or orderly endeavour. It is clumsy and untidy, like the humans who come together to shape it as Christ's body here on earth.

A corollary of all this is that statistical analysis will be of little aid to my study. The blunt information regarding churchgoing or religious belief in modern Britain operates in a different register, presuming as it does that the vibrancy of the church can be measured empirically. But just as we wouldn't presume to assess the quality of an individual Christian by, say, the precise number of good acts she performs or the number of people she brings to faith, nor should we expect to uncover anything true about the church by seeking to pin it down and measure it. Brokenness is hard to transcribe. Vulnerability does not lend itself to statistical analysis. Flourishing rarely translates to measurable outputs. Yes, by our fruits are we known, both individually and corporately. But try to count them and you may just find they diminish before your very eyes.

Instead, I propose a simple disposition: to dwell with the basic rhythms of the church, of prayer and praise, witness and fellowship. To uncover that steady beating that is at its core; that is, as Michael Mayne so memorably puts it, the "*cantus firmus*" (enduring melody) by which we live.[4] I shall seek to understand the church by being and becoming *with* the church—that is, by *imagining* it—rather than treating it as an object for forensic study. I hope to get to grips with my subject matter from the inside. After all, as a lifelong Anglican, it would be naïve to think I can do anything else.

Such an approach risks a lack of criticality, an absence of the sort of perspective that can shine a light on the subject and identify its failings. Against this charge I plead guilty. I cannot be objective about this institution that is the very heartbeat of my life. I consider it from the inside. The journey described is one of personal becoming in Christ, just as much as it is about discovering and uncovering some deeper insight about the church.

It is a journey we can travel together, interrogating our experiences subjectively, because they are no one else's but our own, but doing so in sure and certain hope that there is a bigger story, one that has the capacity to draw all of our individual stories together and make us one body and make us whole. That is the story of God's life in Christ, which I believe is the best story of them all, to which the church continues bearing faithful witness. Hence the power of our imagining of it, which is both uniquely ours and shared with others, which is both particular and general, which is both of this world and of a world yet to come.

And to dwell more deeply in that story, first I need to go home.

CHAPTER 1

Coming home

Christ Church, Fairwarp

I am running over ground that is familiar and unfamiliar. The feel of the soil beneath my feet is at once reassuringly normal and rather strange. Over the years, I have grown unaccustomed to the texture of Sussex clay. I no longer expect to glance down and see white dust floating around my trainers but Somerset's orange soil, fresh from the plough. That's the colour of my home now. It has become my normal.

Ask me where I come from, though, where I regard as home, and I'll point to the clay every time. The picture of home that I carry in my wallet is of the house I grew up in: a functional vicarage in the Sussex village of Fairwarp, right in the heart of the Ashdown Forest. More famous as the birthplace of Winnie the Pooh than as a breeding ground for Anglican clerics, it nonetheless shaped my vocation, forming me for a future that, even as a young man, I knew God was calling me into.

So it is to this place that I return in search of spiritual nourishment. I detour for an hour or more from my route to breathe just thirty minutes of its air, to feel the damp bracken against my legs and feast my eyes on the view of the South Downs that stretches from the summit of my favourite hill. I remember noticing that view for the first time upon returning from university. I gasped at its beauty, wondering how I could have grown up surrounded by such splendour and failed to take it all in.

Now, though, I am headed in a different direction, down the hill to Christ Church, Fairwarp: the church in the forest of which my father was vicar for seventeen years. The church that made me, that began shaping me for the kingdom.

I started at the vicarage, for old time's sake. It is odd to return to a place you have known intimately but no longer occupy. Like meeting a former lover. And the geography of the place has changed. There used to be a path that led through the silver birches onto a broad track that would take you close to the church. You could hop through the silvery-purple heather and pass through a kissing gate into the churchyard.

That's how I remember it, at any rate. But try as I might, I can't find the cut-through. I end up running to the main road and following that back down to the church: a lengthy route that feels strange and unsettling. I've never approached the church on foot from this direction before because we lived in the village, down the hill. Already, I feel like a stranger. And this was meant to be a homecoming.

I pause for a moment in the churchyard, noticing how the light still plays on the pale sandstone of the tower, bathing it in a warm, honeyed glow. The path around the building has been laid with fresh gravel, a brighter yellow than I remember from my wedding photos, taken a decade or more ago. There are more gravestones, of course, some bearing the names of people I used to know. Time moves on, and with it we lose all that we once took for granted.

My grandparents are here, their ashes scattered in a tranquil garden of remembrance in the corner of the churchyard. It seemed important to bring them home, even though we'd all moved on by the time my grandmother died. We knew she'd want to be with Grandpa. They always came as a pair.

So, too, is my great-grandmother laid to rest here, buried because she threatened to haunt my mother if she was cremated. She was the first person I remember dying. I was perhaps ten or eleven and didn't go to the funeral. You have to grow accustomed to death in small steps: don't run before you can walk.

My history is woven into the fabric of this place, my identity caught up in the soil. I remember cycling one hundred times around the church to raise money for charity. I remember sitting on the grassy bank outside the vestry waiting for Dad to finish chatting with his churchwarden and being told by a visiting archdeacon, a second-generation priest himself, that one day my son would be the one picking daisies while I disrobed. I remember glancing up at the multi-coloured tapestry behind the altar, depicting Christ's ascension, and wondering what it would be like to be taken up in glory, if the colours would be this vibrant and rich.

I remember standing beside that altar, offering bread and wine for my father to consecrate, watching his hands shape blessings and pouring holy water on his outstretched fingers while he whispered private prayers. I remember staring intently at the wafer as he held it aloft, wondering what I'd glimpse as the light shone through its pale white core. More light, I supposed, as if the brightness were never-ending.

So it proved. The light came in waves, basking my youth in a glow of Christian fellowship and love. I realize now that my parents shielded us from the more challenging features of life in a vicarage, from the midnight calls to attend the sick and dying, the occasional angry backbiting and criticisms, the sense of holding the world's brokenness before God. As I grew older, I discerned the reality: an odd blend of extraordinary good fortune and sublime vulnerability, of power and weakness all rolled into one. That was the moment of my second conversion, I suppose, when I realized what it really means to be a Christian disciple, called to serve God in the midst of a fragile world. When I realized that village cricket is only a part of the story of parish life. That frailty and weakness come with the package, too.

It took time to wrestle with the angels, to tease out the truth of my vocation in Christ. And then I summoned the courage to respond, risking rejection even while I felt certain I had finally owned up to my destiny, yielded to my identity. That is the paradox of this vocation: it feels like the most natural thing in the world to be a priest, at the same time as feeling strange and occasionally undesired. This is one of the many paradoxes Dietrich Bonhoeffer describes as the "cost of discipleship",[5] a common experience for all of Christ's followers, with the only difference being that it is perhaps magnified for those called to serve as his priests and deacons.

Entering the church, I feel the tension between priest and man all the more keenly. My vocation was certainly instilled in these whitewashed walls, unornamented but nonetheless breathtakingly beautiful to my eyes. Yet, until now, I have never stood in this church as a priest; only as a child, secure in the knowledge that the future is waiting, that I can dwell fully in the present. Even my last visit, as a twenty-seven-year-old bridegroom, was characterized by my reversion to a younger self: Dad was up front in his gold cope, and the ladies of the village cooed over me, as if I were still eleven and had said something clever about the sermon. It was a return to a place of safety, in which I was once known and will always be fully known, but which even then hadn't kept pace with my changing self. I was home, but it felt different. I belonged, and yet I had moved on.

These feelings are exacerbated by the passage of time. I'm in my early middle age now, as the crow's feet around my eyes and greying hair at my temples attest to. I serve my own parishes, churches in which I am the one standing behind the altar, presiding over the weddings and funerals, holding the ring. It is my children who are cooed over now, held in the warm embrace of Christian communities who delight in their presence, even when they misbehave during the intercessions. While the younger version of me is still fully present, his identity entwined with that of the man who kneels now in a pew and bows his head in prayer, there is a new person, a fresh identity that this building has never witnessed, that it could never have known.

Like the white clay on the forest paths, I realize that what was once familiar has become strange: my soil, quite literally, has changed. Christ Church still smells as it always did. The echoes of my footsteps as I explore the Lady Chapel have the same register. The geometry of the building is more or less as I remember. If I were blindfolded, I could have told you where I was and most probably found my way around with relative ease. I remember the rough edge of the font, the smooth wood of the nave altar, the black ironmongery of the simple chandeliers (I remember the flower festival that fundraised for them, too: the smell of the church stuffed full of summer blooms). Dad used to joke at baptisms that children could swing from them if they got bored, though thankfully no one ever did.

Even so, it is no longer my home. It was my place of becoming, once. But places change, people move on. I am not the young man whose identity was formed within these Victorian walls, even though I know him well and carry him within me. Just as the passing of my beloved grandparents signalled a change in my very way of being, because I became shaped by their absence rather than their presence, so the twenty or more years that have elapsed since this was my home have moved everything on: the church, the world, my sense of who I am. To return is nostalgia: an enjoyable trip down memory lane that sharpens my apprehension of the fortunate calling that was first shaped in this place. But it is true what they say: you can never go back. Even if you do, it isn't the same.

Being known

When we gather in church for the Eucharist, our ultimate act of thanksgiving in which we recount Christ's perfect sacrifice that restores the whole creation, we say a prayer that begins with the words: "Almighty God, to whom all hearts are open, all desires known, and from whom no secrets are hidden." This prayer orients us to our encounter with the Trinitarian God who knows us fully. It is a precursor to confession, teeing up our request for forgiveness by reminding us that there's no point hiding from God. He knows us, fully. We can't keep secrets from him.

It is hard to disentangle such knowing from what we think of as our identity, from the phenomena of us. But such phenomena exist in the realm of temporality. They are bound up with things like status and education, with what we project of ourselves to the world. Our journey of becoming is mediated in and through them because we have no other way of navigating through the world.

But what God knows of us is somehow more singular, at once more and less specific. Our hearts are open to him, our desires known. So the transience of our existence, which quickly makes our former selves both familiar and unfamiliar to us, is always underwritten by some deeper knowing, in Christ, which is constant. An enduring melody.

As I stand in Christ Church, I am both fully myself, the same person who stood there on countless occasions for seventeen glorious years, and more fully myself, the father of two, husband and priest who now kneels, looking with interest at the white flecks of clay on his trainers and noticing how they stand out against the orange marks from home. I know who I was. I can see my resemblance to him. Yet I am at the same time aware of how different I have become, even to the extent of wincing at my youthful naiveties, while knowing that I remain unformed. If I return to this place—*any place*—twenty years from now, I will think, too, of how naïve I was back then.

What is it about coming into Christ Church that signifies this uncertain movement between past, present and future? Is it simply that it was the locus of my youthful becoming, that it was a place in which I experienced with intensity the sense of temporality that is a feature of our creaturely existence? Would a non-churchgoing friend feel the same about returning to their childhood rugby club or horse-riding stables? Are my feelings just to do with the passage of time between youth and middle age? Or is there something deeper, cutting to the very heart of identity, that can only be given expression in the walls of a sanctified building in which the Eucharist—that meeting of heaven and earth—is celebrated regularly, in which people express their longing to be known, fully, even while they are fully known?

The feeling prompted by a return to childhood haunts is nostalgia: recognition of the places that made us and a longing, perhaps, to return to the simplicity of self that was a feature of such time. Wry amusement at how far we've come and how far we still have left to travel. But then we move on, either reassured or unsettled by our experience of going back to the past but knowing that we can leave it in a box, unopened if it's painful or occasionally dipped into if it brings joy. These riding stables are where I spent hours turning the dung heap; that rugby club is where I lost a tooth in a hard tackle. And so it goes.

The church, though, is where I glimpsed the self that I inhabit even now, recognizing that it is yet to be transcended, yet to be made whole. There is a curious sense of reaching back and forwards at the same time, to who we were, via who we are, to who we are becoming. So this moment, just this moment, in Christ Church has a uniquely explicatory power. It both unsettles and reassures me, feels both familiar and unfamiliar, because, in that place, I recognize that I somehow knew I would always be this man standing here at the same time as having little clue as to who I would be next.

This growth of self is what it means to be a Christian: to understand that our identity now is always caught up in our longing for the future. To understand that our identity in Christ runs parallel to who we think we are and yet the two are inseparable. We can only know by reference to what we perceive and project of our selves, even while longing for that deeper knowing that is glimpsed in worship, when heaven meets earth and we take our place in the kingdom. Our selves are both familiar and unfamiliar, *even to ourselves.*

The church, it seems to me, mediates such perception because it is the place in which we participate, willingly and through habit, in a shared expression of longing. Through liturgy, our worship, we give expression to our heart's desires, glimpsing what it is to be known, fully, in Christ.

Familiarity and unfamiliarity

The movement between familiarity and unfamiliarity shapes Christian liturgy. And since liturgy shapes our very existence and is enacted for the most part in church, it is perhaps inevitable that the church encapsulates this tension, holds it within its walls and helps us orient ourselves towards it, even when the liturgical act is finished. Think of T. S. Eliot's thought in "Little Gidding" when he speaks of visiting a church and kneeling at the intersection between time and eternity.[6] This is the crux: in liturgy, which is the church's decisive practice, we glimpse both the present and the future, bound up in the past. We see who we are and who we're becoming, bound up with who we have been. We are fully known, even as we wait to find out who we are.

As Eliot discerns, liturgical gesturing between time and eternity seeps into the walls of our churches. Gesturing of this sort actually shapes the world. It is about more than just acts being performed by human beings for their own sake. The liturgy is drama, but that doesn't make it unreal.

That seems to be the force of the philosopher Giovanni Maddalena's notion of "complete gestures", which he explores in a book entitled *The Philosophy of Gesture* (2015) and which he regards Christian liturgy and creative acts of the imagination as exemplifying. He describes various actions that human beings perform that have the capacity to transcend the performer and create meaning in and of themselves. The key thing is that such gestures have a general meaning, which is to say they tell us something *general* about the world and our place within it. Despite this characteristic of generality, they also relate to a *singular* object, such as a given time and place (a church, say), a particular group of people (a congregation) or an individual person. Moreover, these actions express "different possibilities of forms and feelings": they are, that is to say, simultaneously highly specific and open-ended, closed and generative, familiar and unfamiliar.[7]

Now we know why the force of Christian witness is sensed even in an empty church: because it is expressed in gestures, which hang in the air like smoke from a snuffed candle, lingering and shaping the future, even as they signal the past. At a superficial level, that coheres precisely with my experience in Christ Church. I remember being here and take solace in knowing the place intimately. Yet I have moved on to inhabit different possibilities, different forms and feelings. As the fresh gravestones in the churchyard bear glorious witness to, even our ultimate possibility of not-being-in-this-world is a realized outworking of the gesture of becoming that we share in church. That is what the Ash Wednesday liturgy—with its sobering "Remember you are dust and to dust you shall return"—signifies. Not-being is always our possibility and one that, when fully realized, transcends all of the other possibilities that lie open before us.

This, then, is the truth of the church: as an object and an idea, inhabited in community with faithful disciples, it is oriented towards that which is known and unknown: the kingdom of God. It will always be a place of longing and uncertainty, a place that unsettles us even as it calls us home, because it occupies a liminal space, somewhere between heaven and earth.

Rowan Williams, following Victor Preller, puts it more succinctly: "The intellect is oriented to a reality it cannot know."[8] What he means is that our limitations as human beings preclude us from fully living in the kingdom and therefore being fully ourselves—in this life, at least. What he doesn't mean, though, is that we know nothing of God's kingdom and therefore of ourselves—that it is entirely beyond our understanding. Rather, as St Paul reminds us time and again, and most memorably in 1 Corinthians 13, we glimpse it fleetingly, have flashes of inspiration seen "in a mirror, dimly". It is no surprise this reading is so popular at weddings and funerals. All the stuff of life is right there, expressed in the most beautiful poetry imaginable.

What we know of God and his promises to us is perceived only by reference to our dwelling in the world, in the particularity of our context and the identity we inhabit in that time and place: now as a teenager in Christ Church, Fairwarp, now as an adult in Somerset. And so it goes. We glimpse the kingdom through gestures, which are always human and this-worldly, using tokens of our creaturely existence like water, bread and wine, flame and incense. They are located in the *here and now*. The church is the locus of such gesturing. It is *where we do it* together. There is no other form. Small wonder, then, that the church becomes a place of familiarity and unfamiliarity. It is where we put ourselves in the way of that knowledge that is God's promise to us, of being fully known, embedded in this particular time, in this particular place. Yet we soon come to understand that we don't really know ourselves, except fleetingly. We glimpse that which is ultimately true by reference to that which is changing: familiar now, but with the inevitability of becoming unfamiliar as we grow away from it.

So the church curates that glimpse of the kingdom that is as much as we can hope to perceive in our earthly lives. Since that knowledge is both subjective and objective—of ourselves and of God—it will always be partial and incomplete. As creatures, we are always on the move—now in Somerset where the soil is orange, now in Sussex where it is pure-white clay. In church, though, we glimpse something of *who we really are*, mediated always through the particularity of who we are *today, this week, this year*. Which is why when we go back to a place where once we worshipped, it feels both reassuringly familiar and also disarmingly strange. We were fully known then, but now we are fully known.

And that, itself, is question begging. Does this experience I have been describing rely on familiarity with a *particular* church, even if not the depth of familiarity that I have with Christ Church? What happens when the church itself is a place of strangeness, of unfamiliarity? Do we still glimpse the tension between our temporal identity and our identity in Christ? Do we still gesture? To find an answer, I need to go to what is unfamiliar, to embrace the strangeness of the kingdom in a place that I don't know rather than one I do.

CHAPTER 2

Time and eternity

Holy Trinity Church, Geneva

We need to rewind the clock, go back in time. Before Somerset but after Fairwarp. When I was young, and everything was unfamiliar. When my identity was less settled, and I apprehended every day that I was a work in progress, as yet unformed.

Join me now in an Anglican church miles from home. Between the lake and the station, Holy Trinity is the point of connection with the Church of England for expats and visitors to Geneva. A taste of home even when you are abroad. The familiar in the unfamiliar. I find my way here early in the morning, the day of the Motor Show. It is my first big job as a fledgling motoring journalist, all expenses paid. But I am unsettled. The night before was unpleasant: boorish hacks bragging about their career achievements, competing for attention, desperate to mark their territory, to show each other who was boss. This world seems dark, self-interested, narcissistic. I am bruised, out of my depth. What is this path that I have chosen?

Rising at dawn, I feel my way into that which is

familiar. Holy Trinity is a short walk from my hotel. I didn't plan to find it when I set off, hoping only to reach the shoreline of the lake and breathe some fresh, healing air. But when I see it rise before me, testing the door and falling into the peace of its interior, I understand that this is where I was always headed. It is where I knew I would end up.

The details are sketchy. Unlike Christ Church, where my life played out on an almost daily basis for many years, I have been here once, for ten minutes. Most of that time was spent with my head bowed in prayer. I can tell you nothing of the geometry of this building, of the placement of the font or pulpit, if it has ornate chancel carvings or a decorated nave altar. I can't tell you how the light falls. I can report only how I felt inside its walls, reassuringly heavy and familiar. I felt cocooned, at peace, as if this was why I'd come to Geneva: not to write stories about the latest Ferrari or Fiat but to spend ten minutes in prayerful contemplation of the Lord. It's a long way to travel, just to go home.

Here, the feeling of familiarity and unfamiliarity is reversed. The telescope has been turned the other way around. Whereas in Christ Church I can tell you every detail of the place, every detail of who I was in the midst of it, here I can tell you only that I feel reassured, even though I barely recognize myself, let alone the fabric around me. This apprehension that I have been describing of both knowing and unknowing obtains even here. Within the walls of Holy Trinity, I am known in Geneva, even while I am a stranger.

So it seems as if this experience has little to do with my geographical location. It turns out I can feel fully known, fleetingly at least, even when I feel very much out of place. And if this feeling is not about where I am, physically, I think it must be about where I am in time—or, more properly, *out of time*. I feel disconcerted by my experience in Geneva, uncertain of who I am in the company of these people who I claim to want to be like but many of whom I find repellent. So I go to church, am impelled to push open the heavy door of a building I will never know—not intimately, at any rate—and ask for reassurance, for wholeness. I put myself in the way of God's time by entering a place where the kingdom is made known.

As I leave, spirit restored and identity briefly reconfigured (I spend much of the Motor Show in the café reading theology), I can't help but wonder how many others have walked this same path in cities and towns across the world: a path from uncertainty and fear to reassurance and comfort, even if only briefly felt. From dislocation to being reminded of our Lord's tender care. It's akin to the feeling of familiarity and unfamiliarity I have been describing: a complex of emotions all rolled into one, as if time and eternity are fused. As if the future is unfolding even as the past recedes, and the present, with its ongoing concerns, is the only means by which we can apprehend either. By acknowledging our earthly brokenness and seeking God's comfort, we begin the journey of being made whole. We begin our journey home.

Being and time

In the second novel of his elegiac West Country Trilogy, *The Wanderers* (2018), Tim Pears writes a scene of exquisite beauty. I have used it time and again in sermons and in teaching because it seems to me to capture with rare elegance what it is to be a creature caught in time and yet with a capacity to apprehend our transcendence.

Leo, the young protagonist of the novels, is on the road between Somerset and Cornwall. He has been banished from his home. He walks along a ridge with a hermit he has met along the way. In the distance they see rising two unfathomable shapes, drawing ever closer to them with each step. Leo and his companion feel concerned, struggling to work out what's approaching. They realize just as the objects fly overhead, causing them to duck in subdued panic: they are swans, and they fly away behind them.

I think of the movement of these birds as having a unique explicatory power. As they fly away from Leo and his fellow wanderer, they travel into both the past and the future *all at once*: the boy's and the hermit's past, the birds' future. I think of them receding into the future, moving forwards and backwards at the same time.

The philosopher Martin Heidegger captures the sense in which this sensation, caught so brilliantly by Pears, is the very heart of what it is to be human. We are always caught between being and time, he observes (even choosing this as the title of his most famous work[9]), which is to say that to be human, fully, is to be caught in a perpetual movement between past, present and future.

Heidegger had an uncertain relationship with Christianity even though he started off as a Roman Catholic. Despite its brilliance, *Being and Time* does not articulate a sense of an "other" by reference to which our negotiation of time can be configured. There is no clear horizon, that is to say, against which the dramas of our individual lives play out.

In Christianity, though, there is such a horizon. That's the whole point. Time collapses precisely because we exist at the moment in which we perceive past, present and future *at once*—or at least, we come to such a moment through our worship. That moment is the kingdom of God: our destiny and hope, for which we are prepared with a unique intensity within the walls of church. In worship, we glimpse that kingdom and are made ready for it. It seeps into our bones, forming our souls. That doesn't mean the church is the only place in which we glimpse it (it could be on a ridge with a hermit as swans fly overhead), but it does mean that inside a church, any church, we will be uniquely able to apprehend past, present and future in one eternal moment.

That is why, in Geneva, far from home, my identity discombobulated by an understanding that this is not the life I choose, I am given comfort inside the walls of an unfamiliar church, Holy Trinity, in which a story is lived that I know well. I am reminded that this unsettling experience will pass. It is not my whole story, any more than my teenage identity in the walls of Christ Church,

Fairwarp was my whole story, any more than the forty-year-old man typing these words is my whole story. I am a being in time, always becoming, always being remade, always gesturing from past to future. And when that future is, ultimately, participation in God's glorious kingdom, time always plays out against a horizon in which it is made unintelligible, even while it is grasped with rare clarity. The intellect is ordered to that which it cannot understand.

Fundamentally, then, this gesturing I have been describing that takes place especially in church has a twofold character: it is to do with identity in place (as I discovered in Christ Church, Fairwarp, as I perceive now at home in Somerset) and identity in time (as I perceived in Holy Trinity, Geneva). I had to leave home to understand that what the church represents isn't any specific place to me but, rather, the locus of my apprehension of God's kingdom, in which time is made sense of, even while my understanding of it collapses into paradox. To put that differently, the church is a place in which the specificity of my location—now in this place, now at this moment—has the capacity to be transcended, to be made non-specific and general. We are back to Maddalena's complete gestures, towards both the general and the singular. So we move from space to time, from geography to temporality.

A theology of time

It is ridiculous to talk of "a theology of time", for, as I am suggesting, *all* theology holds time and eternity in creative tension. That is its point. Time–eternity is the very essence of the study of God. But even so, it is worth dwelling with the source material. It is worth understanding where we come from in order to establish where we might be going.

So look with me to Karl Barth, the famous Protestant theologian of the twentieth century whose multi-volume *Church Dogmatics* is as compelling as it is inconsistent and impenetrable. One of the reasons his magnum opus has a reputation for being difficult to parse is that it is full of apparent contradictions. Of course it is: he wrote it over many years while he occupied various academic or pastoral roles. It is as much a record of Barth's becoming as it is a work of systematic theology (which gives the lie to the very notion of "system" in theology, of course, while not undermining the value of its pursuit). What is clear throughout, though, is Barth's sense that a collapsing of time in God's life isn't just a feature of Christian living; it is its very essence. When we apprehend God, as we do day by day in our worship of him, we recognize that human time is a mere artefact. God's time is everlasting and stretches across the neat categorizing of human time that we create by parcelling it up (now a teenager in Fairwarp, now a young adult in Geneva, now a middle-aged man in Somerset, and so on).

To illustrate the point, consider what Barth has to say about the status of the Bible in Christian living. In the opening sentences of his commentary on Paul's letter to the Romans, he writes: "Paul, as a child of his age, addressed his contemporaries. It is, however, far more important that, as a Prophet and Apostle of the Kingdom of God, he veritably speaks to all [people] of every age."[10] So the Bible doesn't speak only to the particularity of Paul's community of young Christians in Rome. It speaks as loudly, with as much pertinence, to all Christians, at all times, including to us *now*. Because God is a God of all time, because the kingdom transcends our location in a given era, Paul's words have the power to reach forwards and backwards, to be as true today as they were yesterday and will be tomorrow.

This isn't just an argument about the authority of Scripture, nor does it aver in favour of biblical literalism—quite the reverse, in fact. We can't simply lift Paul's arguments and suggestions from first-century Rome and apply them to twenty-first-century Somerset. Our time has changed. But we are called to live as those who understand how these words shape us, how they form us for the kingdom. We are called to take them seriously, precisely because we wonder almost daily how they can be lived in our context today.

To understand this better, consider Barth's comment in another of his great works, *Evangelical Theology* (1963):

> Theology responds to the Word which God has spoken, still speaks, and will speak again in the history of Jesus Christ which fulfils the history of Israel. To reverse the statement, theology responds to that Word spoken in the history of Israel which reaches its culmination in the history of Jesus Christ. As Israel proceeds toward Jesus Christ, and Jesus Christ proceeds out of Israel, so the Gospel of God goes forth. It is precisely the particularity of the Gospel that is its universality.[11]

Particularity and universality, singularity and generality, familiarity and unfamiliarity. Time and eternity. It is clear that, when we start thinking about the God whom we worship in church, when we ask what it means to live in the midst of his heavenly kingdom, consistent themes emerge: they have to do with the sense in which the now is always only a part of the story. It is the joining of the "now" with the "then" and the "to come" that makes us whole.

The modern theologian David Ford makes a similar point when considering the unsettling mix of precision and vagueness in the risen Christ—the Christ whose presence in and absence from the world configures us for the kingdom. Ford wants to say that the specificity of Christ's historical face matters because it is the means by which we apprehend his reality, his coming into the world as God's incarnate son to cleanse and heal us. But at the same time, he wants to say that there is something "vague" about this face (especially post-resurrection) that communicates its "unimaginable intensity and inexhaustible abundance indicated by the term 'glory'".[12]

Like so much theology, Ford's account strikes us as being *true*, even while we don't quite understand it. Yet the Bible makes sense of it and articulates it with rare economy by addressing the specificity of the times and places in which the risen Christ is seen. Thus Ford:

> In the Gospel resurrection stories there is a strong sense of a disturbance of ordinary recognizability. In Luke, "their eyes were kept from recognizing him" (24.16), and "they were startled and thought they saw a spirit" (24.37). In Matthew, "when they saw him they worshipped him; but some doubted" (28.17). In John, Mary "did not know that it was Jesus" (20.14) and "Jesus stood on the beach; yet the disciples did not know that it was Jesus" (21.4). In each there are verbal and physical signs of recognition but it is clear that, while the risen one is still Jesus, he is not simply the identical person . . . In Mark, the Gospel most reticent about the resurrection, the news that "you will see him" evokes a reaction in the women at the tomb which recalls awestruck worship: "for trembling and astonishment had come upon them; and they said nothing to anyone, for they were afraid" (16.8).[13]

Ford continues with an examination of the Pauline witness, 1 and 2 Timothy and Titus, Hebrews and the Book of Revelation. After this, he concludes:

> So, in practical terms this [underdetermined, vague, resurrected] face [of Christ] is at the heart of an overwhelming diversity of transformations of selves *in worship and in ordinary living*. Intellectually it generates questions which stretch the theological mind and imagination in the spheres of all the classic doctrines.[14]

In worship and ordinary living. This is the rub: our apprehension is configured in and through worship and then shapes our ordinary lives. Who we become while giving thanks and praise, while glimpsing our transcendence even through the specific details of *this church on this day*, is what forms us to be who we are yesterday, today and tomorrow. In church, we are configured for the kingdom. And since, when we worship as Christ's body, the kingdom reaches into the very specificity of our existence, into the whitewashed walls of this church in Sussex or the unfamiliar and unremembered brasses of that church in Geneva, it is of little surprise that we feel its reassuring presence, even when our surroundings are unfamiliar. In terms of the kingdom, glimpsed in the church's worship, we are *always* home.

I think now of the transfiguration, when Jesus Christ takes a handful of disciples onto a mountain and is momentarily clothed in God's glory. Immediately afterwards, face still glowing with heaven's beauty, he steps forwards and touches the disciples, telling them not to be afraid. And when they stand up, relieved that the ordeal is over, all they see is Christ alone, and they know that he is the Lord—not because of the glory just revealed, but because he enters into the particularity of their existence, is with them *now*, reassuring them, touching them, telling them not to be scared.

In Geneva, I am with the disciples, seeking Christ's tender touch, knowing that somehow, this building, this church, this worshipping community, is a locus of his presence for all time and in every place. Barth again:

> The name Jesus defines an historical occurrence and marks the point where the unknown world cuts the known world. This does not mean that, at this point, time and things and men are in themselves exalted above other times and other things and other men, but that they are exalted inasmuch as they serve to define the neighbourhood of the point at which the hidden line, intersecting time and eternity, concrete occurrence and primal origin, men and God, becomes visible.[15]

In this unfamiliar and familiar church in Geneva, in that familiar and unfamiliar church in Sussex, in my home patch of Somerset, I am in that same neighbourhood (an important word), at which the hidden line becomes visible, intersecting time and eternity. It is not a question of place *or* time, therefore, but both. Place and time—and how we hold the two together in the light of eternity. And thanks to a feature of its very structure, the Church of England is uniquely placed to live this paradox, gesturing towards the kingdom now, in this place, and for all time. It is called the parish, the neighbourhood, and it is to this unit of becoming that I now turn.

CHAPTER 3

Parish and particularity

Oxgodby, Yorkshire

A Month in the Country (1980) tells the story of a man who travels to an obscure village in the north to restore a hidden fresco in its parish church. A beautifully succinct novel, it won its author J. L. Carr a place on the Booker shortlist. It stands as one of the most insightful accounts of rural life at the start of the twentieth century. More importantly, it captures the essence of being and time, of memory and becoming. In that respect, it is a story that transcends its own specificity and tells us more fully what it is to be human.

There is a scene, near the start, where Tom Birkin, face still twitching from the horrors of Passchendaele, stands up in the belfry in which he is to sleep during his month in Oxgodby. Behind him is the fresco, hidden by lime and painted over by many generations of puritan clerics. In front is the village and landscape that is to be his temporary home: a place of healing (from the war, from the betrayal of his adulterous wife) and becoming. As Birkin looks out, he sees his surroundings framed by the unglazed window of the church: now this field rolling to the horizon, now those buildings in which his neighbours live.

This moment establishes the form of Birkin's becoming in Oxgodby, of his dwelling in this place. He views the village from the church because, we sense, there is no other vantage point available. The irony is that Birkin is himself a chapel man. The friends he makes are chapel goers and Birkin, narrated as he is by Carr, is less than complimentary about the Anglican church, still less its clergy. But even so, it is by reference to the parish church that he navigates his way through life in Oxgodby. It is the parish that signifies his knowing.

Incidentally, the fresco he uncovers is a judgement, representing the end times. Perhaps that was inevitable, given what we know of the nature of the church. So Birkin is caught, always, between the now of his unfolding life in Oxgodby, the past from which he is emerging and the not yet of the kingdom that is to come. Even as he brushes at flaked plaster with shaking fingertips, reflecting idly on the hope that he will be healed, that his twitch will cease, even as he talks with the villagers who come in one by one to see his work, he is staring at the future, uncovering it before his very eyes.

And all of this in a quiet country church, the like of which we see up and down the country. They may not all have frescos, but they all point to the kingdom. It's in all of their walls, just waiting to be uncovered. And they all provide the frame through which a community is viewed, casting a unique light on the curious combination of people, place and time that signifies a parish. Even if, like Birkin, you're "not church", the parish church is the place in which something is held, some representation of your individual becoming and that of the whole community. The parish church curates time and place in a unique way, for the good of all around.

Greendale, Cumbria

Move with me from the sublime to the ridiculous, from Oxgodby to Greendale: home to the country's most famous postman, Patrick Clifton ("Pat" to his friends), and his cat, Jess. Anyone who's sat with young children to watch this show will know there are three clear iterations of Pat's world. They mark the passage of time, telling the story of rural life in England over the latter part of the twentieth century with peculiar and unsettling economy.

First is the original. Pat lives in Greendale with his wife and son. He rarely leaves the village, with the mail arriving at Mrs Goggins's Post Office for him to deliver. The narrative arc of each episode is the same. Pat encounters a difficulty that threatens his delivery: a cow blocking the road, perhaps, or a flat tyre on his van. One of the local characters (Alf the farmer, say, or Ted the handyman) steps in to help. The mail must get through. Village life is characterized by mutuality and cooperation. Everyone has time for everyone else. They know each other well and pull together to get things done. Time moves slowly. Pat chats to his customers, often stopping for a cup of tea and a gossip. Step into residents' houses, and more often than not you'll hear the clock ticking, marking the slow passage of time in the idyllic village that is Pat's home.

Things have changed by the time we meet Postman Pat Mark Two. The focus of his activity remains Greendale, but there is more mention of Pencaster, the nearby town that is now the local mail centre. Pat still visits Mrs Goggins, but their conversations are briefer, more hurried. There's a sense of increased pressure on the postman. Every episode is played out against an invisible ticking clock: not the one we used to hear in the locals' houses (that's long since disappeared) but one that seems to hang over Pat's head, ensuring he always feels the pressure to deliver on time. And here's the thing: he has become somehow more insular, more self-reliant. If he encounters a problem on his round, he's more likely to fix it himself. Alf and Ted are busy trying to keep their businesses afloat. Pat passes through their lives, but his identity is no longer so bound to theirs. A distance has been created. There are fewer cups of tea slurped between deliveries.

By the third iteration, *Postman Pat: Special Delivery Service*, things have got even more pressured for Pat. He is now based in Pencaster but must be grateful at least still to have employment. His focus is on special deliveries: one-off items that the residents of Greendale have presumably ordered online. They don't have time to visit the shops anymore.

Nor do they have time to chat with Pat, still less to help him if he encounters problems along the way. That's not usually a problem. Pat now has a fleet of vehicles, including a helicopter and an off-road truck. There's not much that technology can't solve. But Pat seems somehow hollowed out, as if his sense of identity has been disrupted. He's no longer shaped by Greendale. It's just where he happens to live, where he rests his head at night and goes from in the mornings after a snatched breakfast and an even more snatched conversation with his wife and son.

There are, though, two constants across all three manifestations of Pat's life: Jess the cat, of course, and another, whose presence is often fleeting but always keenly felt. The Reverend Timms is a vicar straight out of central casting. Balding head, steel-rimmed glasses, a permanently distracted look upon his face, as if he's contemplating higher things. But there's one place where you can still hear the ticking clock, where there's still time for a warming cup of tea and a decent conversation. It's inside his vicarage, where time appears to stand still—or ensue at its own pace, anyway. And his church still stands at the heart of village life. It is where the children start their adventures from, where locals congregate on the rare occasions that they're able to stop and catch up. It's just about the only bit of Greendale that hasn't changed, as if it's curating a different world, a different time. As if it's holding onto some different story about what it is to be human, to live in community, even while the world is eroding our very sense of who we are. It symbolizes a different story about what it means to flourish. It's not about having a choice of vehicles at your disposal or a technology-enabled job in the nearby town. It's about being embedded in community, being able to hear the ticking clock. It's about living in a different time.

Rotherfield, Sussex

My favourite book is entitled *Three Mile Man* (1980). It's an obscure volume, usually available in fits and starts in second-hand bookshops, especially around Sussex. Written by Alan Thornhill, it tells the story of Peter Warnett, a man who rarely left the confines of his community, who knew every inch of the three-mile radius around the village of Rotherfield with a rare intimacy. With beautiful photography and eloquent prose, the book is a detailed telling of the nature of this place. It recounts with care the rhythms of life in its hedgerows and woodlands, its fields and farmyards. But, of course, it is so much more than a work of natural history. It is the telling of a place, of a moment in time, of a being in time. And how does it begin? With this phrase, the most revealing of the whole book: "The glory of Rotherfield village is St Denys' church."[16]

Even amid the glory of our created order, the swooping swallows of summer and the gruff badgers of the evening gloom, the kingfishers bringing colour to the village stream, the hushed calm of Nap Wood in autumn's annual shedding, the *glory* of this place is its parish church, which stands at the very heart, presiding over the rhythms of life, the comings and goings of the swallows, the births, marriages and deaths of its human inhabitants. It is St Denys' that curates time, making sense of everything that happens in the village. It is the curious joining of place and time, of *this place* and *these times*, that is contained within its Saxon walls and which always transcends them, pointing away from the particularity of this context to something transcendent, universal, always beautiful and always true: glory, no more and no less. The glory of Rotherfield.

Places of paradox

As St Denys' is to Rotherfield, so is the parish church to every village and town across the nation: its glory.

As the Reverend Timms and his church are to Greendale, so are every parish priest and their church to villages throughout England: the curators of a different way of being.

As the parish church in which Birkin sleeps and works is to Oxgodby, so is the parish church to each community it serves: the locus of becoming, the means by which its narrative is framed in light of past, present and future.

Each in their own ways, across different times and styles, appealing to vastly different audiences, these imaginings of the parish church tell us something vital: it is a place that, uniquely, holds particularity and temporality in creative tension with generality and timelessness. It is, as I have been saying, the meeting place of time and eternity, familiarity and unfamiliarity, memory and becoming. It is where heaven is glimpsed from earth, where the incarnate Christ is made present to the world. Where the as yet unseen kingdom is made known.

Such could be said of any church, I suppose. But there is something about the *parish church* in particular that focuses attention, bringing the whole world into the glorious light of God's love. The parish church, the Church of England made present in every community, is not just there for the holy few who huddle in its pews. It is there for everyone, the whole community. It is, properly, *our church*, and the very form of the parish encapsulates that with breathtaking elegance.

I like to tell my students that the Church of England came into existence as an outworking of God's providential care of the world. It's a grand and deliberately provocative statement, but just consider the details for a moment. Its origins lie in the odd coincidence of two quite discrete sets of circumstances: a theological reformation in Europe and a belligerent English king who wanted to escape the controlling authority of Rome. We might characterize this as a congruence of theology and politics, of heaven and earth: things eternal and things temporal.

Already, then, we see a history unfolding that is distinctive, in so far as it holds in tension two apparently quite different concerns. On the one hand for a broadening of theological teaching in the church universal, and on the other for a reclaiming of authority for a particular country, caught in a particular moment in time.

Let's consider the theological first. It stems from the concerns of people like Martin Luther, Huldrych Zwingli and John Calvin: theologians of the sixteenth century who wanted to rescue salvation from the hands of an imperialist church that didn't seem interested in the doings of everyday people. It's an oversimplification, but the fundamental theological difference between the Romans and the reformers hinges on the means by which we fallen creatures are saved. Is it through participation in the life of the church and adherence to its rules (and its ruler) or through faith in Christ, redeemer of the world, through whom entry to the kingdom is gained? Is the church the only gateway to heaven or the means by which God's freely bestowed grace in Christ is best apprehended and lived in the light of—the means, that is to say, by which God's grace is *made known and accessible to all*?

The difference can be expressed by reference to another fault line: between the Roman love of liturgy, especially confession, absolution and Eucharist, and a sense among the reformers that God could be apprehended without an intermediary—or, rather, without one other than Jesus Christ, the God-man in whom we are restored to a right relationship with our Father in heaven. And the means by which we apprehend Christ, distant as we are from his life and presence in first-century Palestine, is principally the Bible, which bears unique witness to him and which local churches are called to live in the midst of. Later Protestants would describe the Bible not as God's revelation of Godself, which comes in Christ, but as our only means of apprehending that revelation. When you stop and think about it, that pretty much amounts to the same thing in terms of our knowing.

So the difference isn't just about how we are saved. It's also about the very practices that constitute the Christian way of life: the hallmarks, if you like, of discipleship. If the Roman Catholic tradition from which the reformers longed to break free was about human striving for God's grace, understood as adherence to the church's rules, the reformed tradition was about God's grace coming freely into the world in Christ—and we humans having the wit to discern his presence and respond accordingly through faithful praise and witness.

These theological differences play out in all sorts of other ways, too, including in our understanding of the Eucharist and the sacraments more generally. But it is the odd and timely confluence of their expression with the circumstances of the English king that led, precisely, to the coming into being of the Church of England. In 1534, Henry VIII broke with Rome in a decisive act that fulfilled his twofold wish to divorce Catherine of Aragon and free himself from papal authority. The Act of Supremacy was, then, a political act, but it was undergirded by an emerging theological worldview without which it would have been impossible. In other words, the very existence of Anglicanism involves the merging of the stuff of the world with the stuff of God's life in Christ.

Let's pass over the topsy-turvy character of the period caused by the Catholic Queen Mary's accession after the death of her half-brother King Edward (Henry's longed-for but short-lived son), itself followed five years later by the reign of the resolutely Protestant Queen Elizabeth I. Countless history books cover that ground. Consider instead the repeated patterns that lie at the heart of the Church of England, that are its very essence: (i) democratization of the Bible and Christian liturgy, making both accessible to all God's people, with the church seen as an intermediary to encourage faithfulness; (ii) the articulation of a distinctive theology that held in tension the concerns of the European reformers and those of Rome to balance a commitment to Scripture and sacrament that is not found elsewhere; and (iii) an innate understanding that paradox is at the very heart of the Christian way of life, located uniquely in a Church of England that is *both catholic and reformed*.[17]

That such a paradoxical expression of the life of faith already had an equally paradoxical structure in which to be given expression makes it all the more compelling as a story of God's will for the created order. The Church of England consists of a network of parishes embedded in the very heart of communities in which real people make sense of their individual stories day by day by setting them into the wider narrative of God's life in Christ, revealed through word and sacrament and lived in the church. There could perhaps be no better means of transmitting the notion of a church that is of both the catholic tradition, and therefore concerned with the universal expression of belief that is the same *always and everywhere*, and the reformed tradition of localized expression in the lives of normal people.

In other words, the parish is part of the very givenness of England's structure: a nation that is both whole and fragmentary, that has a cohesive national identity which is always fleshed out in localized ways. The church that serves that nation both derives from, and shapes, this very pattern of existence, holding the general in tension with the particular all the time and understanding that it is through such tension that we are fully made.

For the reformers, it was always the same Bible being read in our vernacular tongues. The same universal truth of a God who loves the world so much that he steps into its mess and muddle and makes it whole. And for the *Anglican* reformers, not least Thomas Cranmer, arguably the most important architect of that reform, who wanted to safeguard the sacramental way of life inherited from Rome, it is the same symbols that gesture both universally and in particular ways to that God, simply because they are the means by which we apprehend the truth of the incarnation: both for all time and in a particular place, at a particular time. That is why Cranmer wanted so badly to create "common" prayer: because he saw that liturgy that is expressed locally has the capacity to convey the sense of a God who steps *into our midst*, in all its particularity, at the same time as gesturing beyond itself to God the Father in heaven.

In other words, the structure of Anglicanism, its network of parishes that are always local, always particular, is a natural outworking of its form and of the content of its beliefs. This is a church uniquely capable of withstanding paradox and polarity: reformed and catholic, local and national, particular and general—because its very essence is paradoxical and defined by polarity. A fragment of the fragment yet somehow also whole.

I want to hold onto this notion of a church that finds unity in diversity. It will be important later. But for now, let us return to the twin notions of place and time. For, together, they are the measure by reference to which the parish is most usefully understood.

Places of becoming

Imagine standing in a place that is geographically specific yet also has the characteristic of generality, making it possible to look beyond the details of context that surround you and apprehend something of the world that is true always and everywhere. Such a place would necessarily be one of liminality, where the normal categories of existence seem somehow to collapse. You would feel as if you were standing at some kind of threshold, between this world and another, this place and all places. Standing, that is, between time and eternity.

There is such a place, in pretty much every community throughout England. We call it the parish, and it is the embodiment of that paradoxical outworking of God's providential care of creation that I've been describing.

It finds its keenest expression in the building that is its heart: the parish church. This is where the very notion of a parish is made sense of, as a unit of becoming in which particularity and generality, time and eternity, familiarity and unfamiliarity meet. It is the neighbourhood of our becoming, the point at which the hidden line intersecting human beings and God becomes visible, fleetingly. It is always a place, a neighbourhood, a particular. Yet it is always much more, the embodiment of a universal truth that is apprehended wherever you kneel, whatever the soil beneath your feet.

What matters is that it is the church in the midst of a community, always gesturing, always faithful to its call, always making present the incarnate Christ. It is always a particular, even if it isn't your particular. It is always a place, *this place*, where we stand *today*, knowing that it represents *all places, always*. Put simply, the parish is where the specificity of time and place uniquely merge and then take us beyond our context, in ways we do not fully understand but which have something to do with the givenness of this very structure to which our buildings bear witness and with the theology they seek to embody. Here we apprehend something that is beyond place and time: the kingdom of God, to which we are called in and through our particularity. If the parish is the unit of our becoming, the parish church is the place in which we focus our gesturing between past and future, in the present, and express our longing to be saved.

That is why the parish church is the frame through which Birkin views Oxgodby, the place in which a different rhythm is curated in Greendale and the glory of Warnett's Rotherfield. It is the place and moment which enables us to transcend the particular, even while we are thrown ever deeper into its grip. And even when we step from this particular, when we move around the country or even around the world, we recognize the gesture, as if by instinct, and know that we are home. We are in the right neighbourhood, even if it isn't our own.

All of which invites a further consideration. In an era when place is less important in the lives of many, when work and family cause us to be scattered geographically, to find the notion of having roots in a given place unintelligible, is the parish, with all its particularity, outmoded? To answer that question, I want to turn the telescope around again, switching focus this time from the local to the national. For it seems to me as if the Church of England has a representative function in our nation that owes its force to the very local structure and form I have been describing. It is, truly, a national church, *our church*. It exercises a pull on the national imagination, forming our psyches and shaping our dispositions, even if the world it inhabits no longer shares its form. To consider that point, let us leave the comfort of our parish churches and consider a building that could reasonably be described as the nation's parish church, Westminster Abbey, and face the humbling prospect of occupying its pulpit.

CHAPTER 4

Somewhere and anywhere

Westminster Abbey, London

So I am become a cliché. It's not what you know but *who* you know. There can be no other explanation for my ascent to the pulpit of the nation's most prominent church: Westminster Abbey. Were it not for a longstanding contact, a former boss from my first teaching post, I know I wouldn't be here. It's not as if the Dean and Chapter have trawled the websites of theological colleges and headhunted me for the gig. Instead, I suspect my friend has behaved with characteristic generosity of spirit. This will be a fascinating experience for his young protégé. It will be a moment of becoming.

I was at the front of a different cathedral quite recently. But on that occasion I was kneeling, not standing, ready to receive the *charism* of the Holy Spirit, mediated through the bishop's hands as he made me a deacon. And try as I might to take this all in my stride, to seem insouciant as I stroll around the abbey cloisters discussing Hegelian dialectics with a minor canon whose intellect is matched by the sharpness of his suit, in my heart I know this isn't a place where I belong. I am out of my depth: a bumbling rural cleric delivered into the very heart of the establishment. Uniquely exposed. Destined to make a fool of myself.

There are more people in the vestry than I am used to seeing in my congregations. The smells in here are unfamiliar, like meeting a wealthy person and scenting their expensive cologne, so different from your own cheap splash-on Woodspice. Their robes are better cut, cleaner, not bundled into an old pull-along suitcase like mine. Smoothing the creases on my surplice, I try to make small talk with the Dean. I remember that he was at school with one of my relatives, though he seems unenthused by this connection. Some people grow further away from their childhood than others, I suppose. Aware that I am drying up, I eschew ecclesial small talk and focus instead on the patterns of this beautiful building, ornate even backstage, rarely seen by the public.

Witness the panelling on the walls, for example, or the polished parquet flooring. All repeated patterns, expertly curated, reminding me in a strange and unsettling way of Rogier van der Weyden's painting, *The Descent from the Cross*. Remember how, in her grief, Mary's body is arched in an exact replication of Christ's, listing to one side, left arm bent up almost at a right angle behind. The implication is clear, to me at least: this is the pattern of Christian living, of brokenness, handed down from son to mother, from mother back to the world. It is a reversal of the divine gift of incarnation. Now I am broken, so you are made whole. But to apprehend it, to live in the midst of this wholeness, you must be broken, too. You must know what it is to be weak, to know what I have done for you. Spotting my discomfort, the minor canon catches my eye, reminding me that it will be a small congregation by the abbey's standards. Only a couple of hundred.

The trouble is that I don't believe in my sermon. Unusually, I have written out a script. In my own parishes, I speak without notes. I want to break open God's Word in the midst of a community that I know and love. That is the implication of the reformed concern to democratize the Bible: that it understands the church as the locus of shared dwelling in the Bible. As the place where we live it in the heart of our communities, on behalf of those communities, showing them what it is to foretaste the kingdom, to participate in God's life.

But I cannot translate my confidence in this task to such an unfamiliar environment. It's not long since I saw the Duke and Duchess of Cambridge being married here, this very Dean presiding over the lavish service in his abbey. We crowded around our television set, eating barbecued sausages and joking about the grandeur of it all. This isn't my community, then, but the set of a fairy-tale movie about princes and princesses, the focus of the nation's attention in times good and bad. No place for young, wet-behind-the-ears deacons who are barely out of college, surely.

So, last night, with the music from a nearby summer party blaring across the garden, I hunched over my computer in the study and wrote out a sermon. My text is Romans 9, in which Paul proffers Abraham and his progeny as a sign and symbol of God's election of us, his chosen people, sweeping to the past in order to make sense of his audience's present by holding out to them the prospect of the kingdom to come. I feel I have something to say on this subject, but the magnitude of the occasion is somehow constraining me. I have lost my chutzpah, my derring-do. The imposter syndrome that is part and parcel of this life I choose has bubbled to the surface, disabling me just at the moment when I need to be on top of my game.

Of course, I haven't told a soul. My parents and Sarah, proud as we steered into our allocated parking space in Dean's Yard, think I have this covered, that I fully expect to be preaching in Westminster Abbey, that it's just what you do. My former boss, who's seen me both in and out of my depth intellectually, surely knows I'm not myself—or at least, not the self I would choose to be on this occasion. But there's been plenty of water under the bridge of our friendship in the years since we moved in opposite directions: him to Westminster, me deeper into the West Country. The last time I saw him was when I stayed in his lodgings after a dazzling night in the press bar of the Houses of Parliament, still dizzy from the experience and barely coherent. I can see that he wonders if I haven't changed rather with the passage of time. Maybe even lost my touch, if I ever had it. So I am alone with my fears, having only the deposed Christ of van der Weyden's imagination for company.

Then it is time. As the post-intercessions anthem ends, I follow the verger's brass-topped wand to the mighty pulpit steps and ascend, heavy country soles resounding against the woodwork, marking it with orange soil. I reach into my creased cassock pocket for the folded script but can't shake a line by the poet and essayist Mary Oliver from my mind: "The best use of literature bends not toward the narrow and the absolute but to the extravagant and the impossible."[18] On an impulse, I discard my script, realizing that it constrains the text, constrains me, reaching as it does towards the narrow. But this letter of Paul to the Romans, this Bible in which it is contained, this faith to which it bears witness, is extravagant and impossible, not narrow and absolute. And it is the same extravagance that we witness in our quiet country churches as in the grandeur of Westminster, surrounded by friends from our neighbourhood or peering down at the faces of MPs and media big hitters, the London elite. The extravagance isn't contained, either in the smallness of our parish churches or the vastness of this national church. It cannot be contained because it is the extravagance of an eternal God who is for all time yet takes the trouble to enter into the precise conditions of our life and draw us ever closer into his life, into his embrace, into his kingdom.

At least, that's what I try to say, in halting, less-than-fluent words. The long-abandoned script flutters from the pulpit halfway through, but I manage a last-second grab to save the battered Bible that has become my only reference point. No one moves to retrieve the folded sheet of A4, aware that I have long since left it behind, that the words are now irrelevant. I hope no one reads it later, seeing its neatness, the careful crafting of its phrases and the weighing of its metaphors and illustrations. They might wonder what they missed.

The benefit of evensong is that the sermon comes right at the end, so I am soon back amid the parquet and panelling of the vestry, acknowledging the polite praise of the procession party. After this, by the west door of the abbey, a frail man grasps my hand and looks at me with determined eyes. He is clearly unwell, old before his time. The damp on his palms shows the cost of coming. Something has resonated in my unrefined ramble, given him strength for the days ahead. Something about extravagance, about a love that is uncontained by any place but lives for all people and for all time. It is, I think, the love of Christ coming down from the cross, handed to Mary in her grief and made human in the very specificity of her sorrow. Extravagant love, never contained yet somehow apprehended through participation in a structure, a repeated pattern, all too human, that is always found *where we are today*. A gesture, as real here in Westminster as it is in my evensong at St Peter's, Ilton, with four people and a dog, because it corresponds to the same extravagance, the same love. It is just the locus of its transmission that adjusts according to the particularity of our place. We are in the same neighbourhood, even when we inhabit different parishes.

Finding somewhere

This, I think, is the nature of that pattern I have been describing: a network of parishes that are somehow replicas of each other in their rhythms of prayer and praise, in the biblical narrative they choose to inhabit, yet at the same time always vernacular, always particular and local. Mary is always Mary, even when she is shaped on Christ. The parish, then, is not only a glorification of the local. It is, at the same time, a means of participating in something that will be perceived as true, as recognizable, wherever we stand or kneel in prayer. The familiar in the unfamiliar, extravagance in this place, today, with these people. That is the neighbourhood in which the parish resides.

That is why valuing the parish church is far from idolatry, still less a fetishization of bricks and mortar. Rather, it is recognition of the precise locus of our becoming. It derives from a sense that everyone longs to belong, somewhere, or, even if you don't buy that line, that we cannot but be somewhere, even if we define ourselves by our willingness to be anywhere.

Such language invites consideration of the popular thesis put forward by the public intellectual David Goodhart in *The Road to Somewhere* (2017). Published in the months after the UK's decision to leave the European Union, it explores how notions of belonging play out in citizens' political judgements, in their very way of being in the world. Goodhart supposes a dichotomy between "anywhere people" and "somewhere people". The former may seem most problematic for my thesis concerning the enduring pull of the parish on our imagination, since they refuse to be defined by their belonging to a particular place. As happy in Beijing as Brighton, Honolulu as Hong Kong, these educated, privileged people expect to have no roots, to move from place to place as work and life demand. If the job or a personal relationship necessitates a move to Berlin, so be it. Home is wherever you hang your laptop case.

Somewhere people, meanwhile, define themselves by reference to place. It's not so much that they put down roots as that they grow from them. They are like the Reverend John Ames, the protagonist in Marilynne Robinson's *Gilead* (2004) who in his youth doesn't understand that the horizon stretches beyond what he can see but always provides the only reference point by which to navigate. So it stands to reason: with narrower horizons comes a narrower worldview. Place becomes not just important but the very means of self-definition.

Put to one side for a moment any reservation about the apparent limitations this distinction imposes on those who see themselves as "somewhere people". Let it be said only that we know roots are unconstraining, provided they are well enough watered. For there is certainly something in Goodhart's argument that resonates and poses a challenge. If "anywhere-ness" has become normative (even though it failed to win the day in the Brexit debate), surely we can abandon the parish?

It used to be popular in Church of England circles to speak about believing without belonging. What we meant is that people understood themselves to be Christians, most probably Anglicans, even though they didn't attend churches. But the sound bite fails to capture the sense in which believing is always tied to some kind of belonging—if not to the church itself, then at least to the place in which it is located. To be an Anglican, even a nominal one, is to *belong*. When belonging in this sense erodes, and the locus of belief is therefore diminished, it poses the most pressing challenge imaginable for a church such as ours, deeply embedded as it is in the particularity of parish and place.

Consider Goodhart on London, since that is where we are located at this moment in our discourse. "London," he writes, "is Anywhereville . . . It is a city that has partially outgrown its country and sometimes feels more attached to the rest of the world than to its own national hinterland."[19] Yet here I stand, on the steps of Westminster Abbey, in the heart of the parish of Anywhereville, recognizing the familiarity between here and my obscure Somerset village: a familiarity that transcends details of context while at the same time throwing me ever deeper into them.

If Westminster Abbey is a church for anywhere people, it is so because it locates them *somewhere*. It is my suspicion that this somewhere is the parish of their imagination: the place where, in their hearts, they know they belong.

There is of course a first-order assumption behind this. Namely that anywhere people secretly long to be somewhere people, even if they don't quite know it. Or, at least, that as much as they define their lifestyle by their mobility, they nonetheless have roots which can be traced back, or forwards, to a place of belonging. Even when we are far away, we want to know there is a home to go to. The church provides it.

Westminster Abbey is the nation's parish church: a symbol of every parish church that we have known and will know in our lives, in our communities. When we see royalty married in its walls, we are thrown back or forwards to our own marriages, or those we have attended and will attend, in countless parish churches up and down the land. When we think of its clergy, pressed robes or not, we think of the clergy we have known and will know, praying faithfully in their parish churches, like Reverend Timms in Greendale. The abbey is representative of a truth hardwired into our national psyche because, as I have been arguing, the parish is itself hardwired into our national identity. We fundamentally believe that there is always a place in our midst in which the kingdom of heaven is glimpsed and that our identity is somehow always configured by reference to it.

The clearest exponent of such a view that I can think of is the late Roger Scruton. For example, in *Our Church* (2012), he writes:

> ... we need to recognize that religion is not simply a matter of believing a few abstract metaphysical propositions that stand shaking and vulnerable before the advance of modern science. Religion is a way of life, involving

> customs and ceremonies that validate what matters to us, and which reinforce the attachments by which we live. It is both a faith and a form of membership, in which the destiny of the individual is bound up with that of the community. And it is a way in which the ordinary, the everyday and the unsurprising are rescued from the flow of time and re-made as sacrosanct.[20]

Contained in this quotation is a series of counterpoints to the very notion of anywhere people. It shows that we are always drawn more deeply into place, that we can resist its pull, even as we hop from airport to airport, desperately searching for a Wi-Fi signal. As a bare minimum, we have a memory of belonging which can look both forwards and backwards because it is a memory of the kingdom that is to come. And the Church of England is the means by which we apprehend it, focus our attention on it, dwell in the midst of it.

That is why the whole nation tunes in to watch the royal wedding. It is why the tourist queues outside Westminster Abbey stretch all the way along Victoria Street. It is why there are two hundred and counting at this evensong, right in the heart of Anywhereville. Somehow, the national church participates in the local church. That is the further meaning of the parish. Not only local and particular but national and particular, for everyone a reminder of their somewhere.

The Church of England, with its network of parishes that stretch across the whole country and give local expression to the universal truth of God's extravagant love, is a powerful means by which a nation's imagination is captured. The parish, innately local, is the means by which we apprehend our national character. It is capable of transcending itself in its very particularity and telling us who we are as a people. Moreover, for those who are defined by their lack of a somewhere, a church such as Westminster Abbey stands in for the parish, becomes its representative. The example of Westminster Abbey serves as a reminder that a celebration of the parish as the local manifestation of a national church such as I have been putting forward does not equate to *localism*. Rather, it points to our wider participation as Christian people in society, reminding us that we are always a part of something bigger, a fragment of the fragment. Parochialism, that is to say, is not inward looking, nor is it insular and narrow-minded. Properly understood, our location in our parish, in any parish, reminds us to look beyond the horizon and embrace the dizzying diversity of each local expression of our national identity, held together as they are within a fragmentary body that is also whole.

But, as we know, confidence in our ability to hold unity and diversity in tension has waned. So let us consider its defence, for it is the very heart of the Church of England as I have been describing it.

CHAPTER 5

Though we are many

I have long thought that if the Church of England were personified in a character from twentieth-century literature, it would be Christopher Tietjens from Ford Madox Ford's baffling yet brilliant *Parade's End* trilogy (1924–8). Tietjens is an infuriating man whom we are nonetheless destined to admire, if not actually like. Madox Ford is at pains to signpost his awkwardness, physically and intellectually. A traditional Tory, he falls in love with a suffragette. A committed Anglican, he allows his son (who may not be his son, such is his wife's profligacy) to be brought up as a Roman Catholic. A man with an innate respect for hierarchy, he nonetheless causes those in authority over him no end of trouble, mainly by doggedly behaving as honourably as possible in spite of their wishes.

Those familiar with the novels will know that Tietjens's reputation is often very poor. Rumours swirl around him, often perpetuated by those who find his apparently old-fashioned values hard to stomach. Yet he rarely reacts to the insults: not his wife's cruelty nor when facing financial ruin as a result of a love rival bouncing his cheques at the family bank. Instead, he sticks faithfully to the path that he believes to be right and true: love of one's country, execution of one's duty, living with honour.

It is the faithfulness that gets people, every time. In a wonderful scene, brought to life with great verve in Tom Stoppard's screen adaptation of the novels, Tietjens is berated by his would-be lover, Valentine Wannop, the suffragette, who decries his steadiness, his unwillingness to rant and rave or behave irrationally. It is his calm that she finds unfathomable. Why can't he just show some emotion?

For those who have followed the ups and downs of the Church of England's internal debates about controversial topics such as the moral status of homosexual conduct or the ordination of women priests and bishops, frustration at a lack of emotional engagement is a common experience. Why is every official teaching document couched in neutral language, unwilling to nail its colours to the mast? Why so wary of offending or upsetting the status quo ante? Why can't this church just show some humanity? Why can't it be *real*?

The answer is that being real involves holding paradox in tension rather than reaching for straightforward answers. That is the stuff of life. And to do that in a way that seems rational and considered is inevitably very difficult because paradox is the enemy of rational thought. Just ask Christopher Tietjens or his Roman

Catholic son. You could ask Rowan Williams, too, who has done more than many to articulate the theological basis of the Church of England's holding not of the centre ground, as commonly thought, but of a diversity of views in one holy body.

The point is that living with paradox is very different from the old cliché about Anglicans—that we like to sit on the fence. It's not that we're committed to compromise. It's rather that, for all the reasons I've been exploring in this essay, we recognize that the world is a messy, uncertain place, in which things can't always be parcelled up neatly, in which answers are often far from clear, even in relation to topics about which we long to have clarity.

To take one example, let us consider the vexed topic of human sexuality and more specifically a question that the church seems unable to reach a consensus about: are same-sex sexual relations morally permissible? I long with every fibre of my being to say they are and believe intuitively that they are. But I also believe the Bible to be a source of moral insight, to have authority as the text by reference to which I am called to live. I regard it, for reasons already discussed, as the divine Word my fellow disciples and I are called to inhabit in community with each other. And no matter how hard I try to see otherwise, the Bible takes a consistent line on such behaviour: it is not the ideal for human sexual relationships.[21]

What, then, am I to do? Like Tietjens, having integrity necessitates accepting hypocrisy. I am liberal when it comes to same-sex relationships, even while reading from a Bible that I know is critical of such conduct. I suspend the biblical teaching not for the sake of being pastoral but because I believe, in my heart, as it were, that same-sex relationships have just as much potential as a heterosexual marriage to be life-giving, profoundly beautiful and, yes, representative to the world of God's love for the whole creation. But my position is less than perfect, and I know my personal cost is as nothing compared to that of the people who feel slighted or, worse, are oppressed by the church's historic position on this and many other matters. Which makes me feel worse and yet evermore impelled to occupy a space of impossibility, between yes and no, what I know and don't know.

So the Church of England is a place of paradox. The parish embodies that in its very essence: local and national, somewhere and anywhere, familiar and unfamiliar, particular and universal. The Church of England priest feels it perhaps more keenly than most (a statement that is true a fortiori for the bishop or archbishop). And, of course, as Williams discovered, immediately we try to find words that describe the paradoxes in which we live, we seem circumlocutory, vague, perhaps even shifty. So perhaps we are better just to live them, to dwell in the midst of them, knowing that when words run out, true knowledge begins.

The Church of Christ the Cornerstone, Milton Keynes

We share a moment in the centre of Milton Keynes, the man with the broom in his hand, scrubbing it against the ingrained chewing gum on the pavement, and me. He doesn't know where the church is. He tells me he's worked here for a long time, many years, and no one's ever asked him before. He's not a churchgoer himself, though he does believe in God—or, at least, he thinks he does. After chatting about that for a while, we cast our eyes upwards and notice the iron cross on the dome of the building just behind. Viewing it at ground level, I had thought it was an office building or possibly a branch of a supermarket. But neither of us can think of a high street chain that uses a cross as its logo, so we trust our instincts and head towards its doors. Sure enough, it is the Church of Christ the Cornerstone: an object that may well represent peak Milton Keynes. Modern by design, it's an ecumenical space shared by—deep breath—the Church of England, the Methodist Church, the Baptist Union, the Roman Catholic Church and the United Reformed Church. That's a lot of churches for one space, as my new friend observes before moving off to continue his work, shaking his head that he should have worked in the shadow of such a building for all these years and not realized what it was. *A church indeed.* Whatever next?

I am embarrassed by my traditionalism when it comes to church buildings, but the truth is that the Church of Christ the Cornerstone is not my favourite example of an ecclesial structure. I don't know whether it's the hand sanitizers at every entrance or the functional layout that can be rearranged to suit the needs of each denomination, but it doesn't grab me. Not as a space in which to encounter God in Christ. It's too busy, trying too hard to be all things to all people. I find it difficult to know precisely what it is seeking to embody.

I chide myself for my narrow-mindedness, noting the limitations of my outlook. Surely I don't need ancient architecture to apprehend the risen Lord? It's not about the grandeur of the building or its pretty stained glass. It dawns on me that maybe I am an idolater, after all. But, of all the churches I visit, often simply to sit in quiet contemplation as I seek to do now, this is the one that moves me the least. It is bland, uninteresting, and yet it should be a place of vibrancy and life. Think of the glory of all these Christians, of such varied denominations, using the same space to give thanks and praise to God. Think of the rich potential for seeing God's unity amid the glorious differences in our human worship. Think of the powerful witness, in an age of fragmentation and disunity, of five different Christian denominations putting historic schisms to one side and cooperating for the good of the kingdom.

Yet here I am, hands smelling of disinfectant, and it's hard to pin down a unifying theme, a sense of the *story* of this building. I'm sure those who use it, whose lives are configured by their shared worship in its walls, could tell you that it stands for the power of the Gospel to unite us and help us put aside our differences. But it feels to me as if it reduces the dizzying variety of Christian witness to the lowest common denominator. Rather than celebrating our differences and recognizing that there is no view from nowhere, that ultimately we are all *somewhere* people, it seems to opt for homogeneity, papering over the fissures that are a part of our inheritance. At best, it leads to blandness. At worst, to dishonesty about who we are as a people, as if we don't quite believe what we say we believe. As if the differences between us aren't so real, after all.

So I choose not to linger in this postmodern space, which could be a municipal building in any town or city were it not a church. I don't quite understand why it exists when there are clearly plenty of denominational churches within a stone's throw. Wouldn't it be better to encourage worshippers to these places and be sure to meet regularly in each other's churches in a spirit of ecumenism and mutuality? Isn't it better to stand somewhere, even if it's not quite your somewhere, rather than nowhere?

Making space for diversity

As I have been saying, the gift of Anglicanism is precisely this: that it always stands somewhere, even when it appears to hold the middle ground. Indeed, its beauty is its diversity, the sense that in one fragment of the church universal are contained many fragments:

different expressions of the life of faith and witness that are all true because they all gesture in some way between memory and becoming, between temporality and eternity. It is why a Church of England service can involve anything from incense and football-team-sized altar parties in flowing robes and birettas to tracksuit-wearing worship leaders with drums and bass guitars, for whom sacramentalism is a dirty word. We all know where we stand on this continuum, but we all recognise that we stand in continuity with fellow disciples who we love deeply but with whom we profoundly disagree.

That is the essence of synodical government, which is another distinctive gift of the Church of England, seen too in the structures of some of our closest ecumenical partners. It establishes governance by the faithful, through debate and disagreement, in the hope that through such discourse truth is slowly (sometimes painfully slowly) uncovered. As Paul Avis, one of the most prolific exponents of Anglicanism, writes: "Anglicans are averse, by tradition and conviction, to hierarchical, monarchical and authoritarian methods of leadership and to attempts to impose a monolithic uniformity."[22]

The trouble with a rejection of "monolithic uniformity" is that it is hard to commentate, let alone present to an increasingly soundbite-driven world as unity rather than fragmentation or muddle. But the Church of England is *always* disagreeing with itself, as many of my non-churchgoing friends observe. It's always debating some big issue or other and making a mess of it by failing to reach a conclusion: marriage in church after divorce, homosexuality, women bishops—and so the list grows. The church has been in a perpetual muddle about these and a range of other issues for as long as any of us can remember.

Their point is that, somehow, through its perceived unwillingness to reach a consensus and deliver a clear message on a range of topics, through compromises like the apparently muddled teaching on human sexuality that says homosexuals can be together, apart from when they can't, or the teaching around ministry, which says that women priests and bishops are fine, apart from for those people for whom they're not, the church doesn't do itself justice. It would be better if it could just be clear about where it stood rather than fudging everything. Even if we disagreed with it, at least we'd respect it.

What my friends don't realize, though, is that the Anglican way isn't about clarity or indeed consensus. Yes, synod is democratic and formulates teaching and church law by reference to the will of a (sizeable) majority. But even then there are exceptions, ways to hold the ground for those who simply can't act in accord with the rules. Take the conscience clause relating to marriage in church after divorce as a case in point. It allows any cleric to refuse to remarry a divorcee in their parish church if their conscience does not permit it. Consider the formulation of that sentence again: it's an opt-out, not an opt-in. Clerics are legally obliged to marry parishioners, including those who are divorced. But if they can't in good conscience do it, perhaps because they know the new relationship played a part in the breakdown of the old one or simply because, in their own mind, marriage is for life, they can refuse.

That's what the Church of England does so brilliantly and chaotically: it holds not the middle ground but a space in which dialogue and disagreement are acceptable, in which nuance and uncertainty are encouraged, in which the judgement of the individual, if held in good faith amid the body of Christ, is valued. In that respect it's not only countercultural but of more fundamental importance to society than ever before. Couldn't we all do with an organization at the heart of local communities and national life that reminds us things are never straightforward? It's never simply a case of yes or no, left or right, leave or remain. It's always all of those things, held in tension, articulated in a spirit of love and mutuality.

The body's becoming

There is a neat anecdote about Rowan Williams in Andrew Brown and Linda Woodhead's acerbic look at the Church of England, *That Was The Church That Was* (2016). It describes Linda asking a devoted fan of "Rowan" what one of his Oxford sermons was about and receiving the reply: "Oh, I don't know. Something about the dark being light and the light being dark. Not sure really, but it was simply marvellous."[23]

In this quotation is summed up not just the essence of Williams's theology, and of his oversight of the Anglican Communion, but the very essence of the Church of England, which he grasps with a rare clarity. Williams has always believed that when we start to talk about anything that matters, we reach what he uses as the title for a memorable but characteristically complex volume: *The Edge of Words* (2014).[24] We become if not inarticulate then at least aware that our language is inadequate. Whether we are talking about the incarnation, the nature of the church, the essence of being, or time itself (as Heidegger realized), we inevitably collapse into paradoxical thinking. We join Leo and the hermit, watching swans on the ridge. We can't fully make sense of what we're reaching for, even as the words tumble from our lips or find form on a page. That's what it is to be human. And yet we rarely shut up (other than sometimes in church or our personal devotions). We hope that by talking, by writing, by praying and singing, we make sense of *something*, even if we don't quite understand what it is we're making sense of.

There is a twofold implication to this. The first, and most crucial, for understanding Anglican ecclesial polity is that we must remain open to the views of others. We must be committed to openness and mutuality, to dwelling with those with whom we most fundamentally disagree. Williams explores this magnificently in an address given to the Lambeth Conference of 1998 (before he was Archbishop of Canterbury) and subsequently published in a paper entitled "Making moral decisions"

(2001). He talks of the diversity of views within the Anglican Church, focusing on different judgements regarding the morality of nuclear weapons as a test case. Making plain his belief that there can be no defence of such weapons, he observes:

> And having said that I believe [it] is impossible [to tolerate or defend the use of nuclear weapons], I at once have to recognize that Christians do it; not thoughtless, shallow, uninstructed Christians, but precisely those who make themselves accountable to the central truths of our faith... I cannot at times believe we are reading the same Bible; I cannot understand what it is that could conceivably speak of the nature of the Body of Christ in any defence of such a strategy. But these are the people I meet at the Lord's table; I know they hear the scriptures I hear, and I am aware that they offer their discernment as a gift to the Body.[25]

Later, he writes of those with whose position he disagrees:

> ... I am forced to ask what there is in this position that I might recognize as a gift, as a showing of Christ. It comes—for me—so near the edge of what I can make any sense of. I have to ask whether there is any point at which my inability to recognize anything of gift in

another's policy, another's discernment, might make it a nonsense to pretend to stay in the same communion.[26]

But he concludes that it is worth the cost, for the disagreement reveals as much about himself as it does about his interlocutors and even more about what it is to belong to this body that we call the Anglican Church:

> When I reluctantly continue to share the church's communion with someone whose moral judgment I deeply disagree with, I do so in the knowledge that for both of us part of the cost is that we have to sacrifice a straightforward confidence in our "purity" ... If another Christian comes to a different conclusion and decides in different ways from myself, and if I can still recognize their discipline and practice as sufficiently like mine to sustain a conversation, this leaves my own decisions to some extent under question ... So long as we still have a language in common and the "grammar of obedience" in common, we have, I believe, to turn away from the temptation to seek the purity and assurance of a community speaking with only one voice and embrace the reality of living in a communion that is fallible and divided.[27]

I have huge sympathy for this viewpoint, no more fathomable for all the care taken in its articulation. This, to me, is the essence of this church to which I belong and which I love with my whole being: for all our diversity, we share practices, the "grammar of obedience". That is what we hold in common. It is what commits us to recognizing our divisions, to acknowledging our brokenness and to longing for that day when we will be made whole in the kingdom. As Williams makes plain with his example of nuclear weaponry, it is precisely when we encounter those views with which we most vehemently disagree that we most readily perceive our brokenness and are therefore confronted by the truth that lies at the heart of faith: we must be open to change. Consider again Madox Ford's peculiar hero Christopher Tietjens, the committed Tory traditionalist and rational thinker who falls head over heels in love with a social activist. It is through what is unfamiliar that we are taken out of ourselves and, if not made able to view the world from another's perspective, made able to at least understand that the conviction with which they hold their views should raise questions for us about ourselves. It is in the face of the other that we most readily see our own needs and so express our yearning for the kingdom.

There is, then (to register the second implication of our knowing and unknowing at the edge of words), an eschatological dimension at work all the time, located for us human creatures at the intersection of earth and heaven. That is why our worship is so important, as are the buildings in which we enact it. As Williams discerns, it is here that we are most confronted by our differences because it is our moment of unity. It is also here that we recognize that our apprehension of the kingdom, our ability to live it now, even though it is yet to come, is linked irrevocably to our willingness to dwell with our differences. It is through this that we recognize our brokenness, our fallenness. This is the means by which we give corporate expression to our longing for God's return, to complete the work of the cross. To not know, and therefore to disagree with each other, is to be human, to beg for Christ to touch us as he steps towards us from glory. Or, to put it differently, if we knew, we wouldn't need to wonder. And where would we be then?

You can tell a story about most parish churches that expresses this distinctively Anglican mindset. Sir Roy Strong does it in a lovely volume entitled *A Little History of the English Country Church* (2007).[28] Open it at random, flicking to pretty much any page, and you'll see how the very buildings in which Anglicans have worshipped for generations were formed out of disagreement about matters temporal and eternal. Church architecture and practice reflect the mores of different eras, hence the high altars in some parishes and the lack of stained glass in others. And anyone who has ministered in a rural church such as the ones Strong describes in his book will tell you how far back a community's memory can stretch. Many are the parishes I have known for whom the Oxford Movement of the nineteenth century feels contemporary, even though it drew inspiration from the liturgical norms and church furnishings of 1549. Such faithfulness to history is itself a mark of the gesturing that takes place in churches between the past and the future by means of the present. So it should come as no surprise that a church which is defined by the nationwide presence of these buildings in local communities, and by the worship that takes place within them, should be characterized by its diversity. It is just another of the paradoxes of the Church of England, which, like all the others, gets to the very heart of this church as a sign and symbol of things to come.

It is the Anglican way, part of its gift, to dwell with difference, honourably and with faithfulness. It is a part of our shared living of the kingdom, of what is to come, in the midst of the communities where we are present: a further sign of the generality towards which our particular gestures reach. Far from problematizing our uncertainties, we should have confidence in resisting the characterization of Anglicanism as neither one thing nor the other. It is, rather, both *this thing* and *the other*, held in holy tension, held together by the Holy Spirit. Our compromises aren't fudges. They are a mature willingness to live with disagreement in our body, seeing it as a sign of the diversity across the whole body of Christ, the church universal, and seeing it, too, as a sign of the weakness from which we yearn for redemption.

I should perhaps feel more positive about the Church of Christ the Cornerstone as I make to pass out of its wheezing automated doors. It is the very embodiment of this willingness to dwell with difference that is of value to the church and to the world, now more than ever.

Far from papering over the cracks of denominational disagreements, it lives in the cracks: it is a giant fissure in the heart of the concrete of Milton Keynes, showing the community there that such brokenness is the very path to our becoming.

Even so, I can't help thinking as I pass through the grey grids of the town centre and leave the church in my past, it could do with a more tangible way of celebrating the diversity of its occupants. That way, at least we'd all know what it stands for.

CHAPTER 6

Growth and glory

A sports hall, the South Coast

I am in the heart of Anywhereville: a sports hall on a Sunday morning, climbing ropes tied back against the wall, furled badminton nets poking out of poorly closed cupboard doors. If I look closely at the polished floor tiles, I can see the marks of trainers: the same black skids, no sign of soil colour to distinguish them one from the other. You'll have worked out by now that I am far outside my comfort zone here: overdressed, just too stuffy for the style of worship unfolding around me. It reminds me of when, as a teenager, I bought tickets to a concert by a dance–metal band called The Prodigy—to impress a girl, naturally. I remember turning up in my chinos and lambswool sweater and feeling mystified that everyone else was in scruffy T-shirts with cut-off sleeves. I remember my shock at entering the baking-hot concert hall and feeling my heart pounding in my chest—not through excitement or fear but because of the sheer volume of the bassline. It was abundantly clear to me and everyone else that I was out of my depth, that I didn't quite belong. I remember thinking that if only I could overcome my natural reserve and throw myself into it, jumping up and down with the dancing hordes and swinging my long-removed jumper above my head like a woollen lasso, I'd get much more from the experience. But I simply couldn't do it: I felt too self-conscious, unwilling to let myself go.

That is how I feel now, and it's a curious thing. We've eaten cookies and consumed liberal quantities of high-quality coffee. Even this is a shock to my system. I'm accustomed to stale digestives and fairly traded brown liquid *after* the service, not before. Usually, I swig the coffee down before racing to my next service a couple of miles away and repeating the process all over again for another dozen or so faithful congregants. Here, though, there is no such rush. We can linger all morning and into the afternoon if we choose. We're waiting on the Spirit, after all.

And the welcome. My goodness, I don't think I've ever been greeted in such a warm way as I set foot inside a church. A gang of young, beautiful people have descended upon me, smiling and happy, eager to please. I feel old, and now I am only in my early thirties. And I feel irredeemably stodgy, as if I'm just too uptight fully to enter into the experience that is to come.

There is plenty of time to warm up, however. As the formal (if you can call it that) part of worship gets underway, it takes the form of a casual coming together of the gathered throng of one hundred or so worshippers. Slowly but surely we set our coffee cups on the tables before us and join in with the praise. After a handful of songs, I wonder how many we will work through before a greeting is uttered and the service proper gets going.

But still we sing, the fervour building as the band gets more and more involved. The music is astonishing: melodic, performed by musicians who have the skill of professionals, and the whole thing choreographed by the band leader, who occasionally issues a call and response to the congregation to help build their anticipation. If I ignore some of the words being projected onto the screen at the front of the hall, I find myself rather enjoying the experience. It's uplifting, after all, to sing beautiful songs in company with lively people who have a tangible love of our Lord. And the structure of the songs, the way the choruses build to a crescendo that reinforces the truth of Christ our saviour, is oddly compelling. Unlike much Anglican hymnody, which condenses complex theological doctrines into pithy phrasing and invites intellectual consideration even as you sing, this is about raw emotion, pure and simple. I sing that I am broken, wounded, sinful, but that I have a saviour who gives me a future, turns my life around, heals my pain. I just need to accept him into my life and devote myself to him.

If the Church of England worship that I am used to works hard to steer a path between the Protestant theology of the reformers and the more works-oriented theology of Rome, this is pure Protestantism: an eschewal of liturgy, of form. Even as I sing, trying to prevent my hands from rising like those of the people around me, I note that I have only one challenge: to accept Jesus into my life, to pattern my existence on him. To be a devoted disciple. Then all will be well for me.

Despite the resistance to form, there seem to be a lot of rules. Some are unspoken, to do with the shape of the worship, which is easily inferred even for a newcomer like me. I have a sense that I know when the Spirit will descend upon us, when the glossolalia will start up. People seem to know when the prayers for healing are needed and when the testimonies to their efficacy will be required. The band rarely strikes up spontaneously but always in response to a cue. Despite the absence of a service book or pew sheet, there's a clear structure to this worship. But, rather like the difference between an Apple Mac computer and a PC, you don't need an instruction manual to discern how it all works. Just follow your instincts, and you'll be fine.

There are other rules, too, about what it means to live a life of faith. Because it turns out accepting Jesus means living a certain sort of life: heterosexual, preferably married and highly fertile, with an unswerving belief that prayer can change the course of not just the universe but of your individual life—that special providence is very much a possibility and comes especially into the lives of those with enough faith. If only you trust enough in the Lord's healing—in his specific ability to change your life and make you whole—then your future is secure.

In spite of the ongoing theological critique bouncing around my mind, I experience a pang of superstition. Has my recently diagnosed illness come because of a lack of faithfulness? Can it not be cured because I don't pray with enough fervour for God to intervene or don't believe, in my deep heart's core, that he will? Judging by the testimonies being shared from the stage, he's helped a lot of people who come here regularly. Is it the case that he's not a fan of my strain of buttoned-up Anglicanism, after all?

Hours pass in this vein, and I wrestle with my conscience. In spite of my reservations, and my reserve, I find the whole experience seductive. I feel as if I could matter to God, and to this community, if only I were prepared to throw myself into it with gusto, to commit fully. There can be no half-heartedness here. Even in this act of worship, I feel somehow insincere for standing back with my hands in my pockets, mouthing the words to songs I don't quite agree with. I feel ashamed of my awkwardness when those around me speak in tongues. I flush with embarrassment when turning down an offer of personal prayer, as if I've come to a party and refused a drink from the host.

By the end, as the mixing desk and drum kit are dismantled and the badminton nets are unfurled for the next group to use, I am exhausted. The faces around me glow, and it is clear that something has been at work here. Rarely do I see such enthusiasm for the Gospel in my parishes. People may remark on a line or two from the hymns, or the sermon, or even the intercessions that struck a chord. But I'm not sure I can remember witnessing anyone's face glowing with the joy of the Spirit as they pass into the churchyard. It's just not our way. And yet, rather like Christopher

Tietjens in his encounters with Valentine Wannop, who pulls at everything he takes for granted in the world, through my experience of this church that is profoundly other—not rooted in place, non-liturgical, relaxed and informal—I see something of profound value. It shakes my assumptions about the nature of worship and the nature of the God whom we worship. It reveals my brokenness. And, finally, knowing that I don't fit in here, I find myself longing for home.

Lost and found

There is a beautiful pairing of poems in William Blake's *Songs of Innocence and Experience* (1789–94)[29] called "The Little Boy Lost" and "The Little Boy Found". They have to do with losing one's bearings and the joy of being found. The first poem describes a child wandering across a deserted fen and calling out to his father for comfort. It ends with the deceptively simple form of this stanza:

> The night was dark, no father was there,
> The child was wet with dew;
> The mire was deep, and the child did weep,
> And away the vapour flew.

In these childish phrases is contained a sense of the horror of abandonment. It makes me think of Christ on the cross, weeping at his godforsakenness, utterly wretched and yet not without hope. Or Mary, replicating his agony in her body as he is lifted down from the cross, passing the pain on to us. The world is dark and foreboding for that child in the deep mire: the vapour (light) has disappeared. We all know what that feels like: we lose our sense of direction, wander aimlessly, often further away from where we need to be. The lights by which we navigate haven't disappeared. It is only that we have moved to a place where we can't see them. We have left behind that which calls us home, often in pursuit of home itself. That is surely the definition of losing one's way: that we are still searching for the thing we most want in the world, and it is that very search which sends us off track.

There are days when I think the Church of England is that child in the mire, desperately calling out for help but wandering further from its very source. We've stopped cupping our hands around the vapour because we're no longer certain it's the right light to be preserving. We look over the horizon and see the bright lights of another neighbourhood, and we can't help but wonder if it's where we should be heading. So we go in that direction, hoping against hope that it will feel like home but knowing in our hearts that we belong in a different place, *our place*: home.

The abandonment of Anglican liturgy in the pursuit of growth for its own sake is a misstep. An understandable misstep but one that could lead to the very demise of that thing we're so desperate to preserve: a church that is for everyone, for every community and the whole nation. A church that can be taken for granted, that has the very great privilege of being a part of everyone's life, wherever they may be: marrying them, baptizing them, marking their passing from the world and, day by day, week by week, bearing faithful witness to the kingdom in the very midst of their communities. A church that is simply *there*, keeping the faith, whose candles can be seen glowing even when there's no one inside, whose presence is writ large locally and nationally, into whose walls we can enter at will and be still, feeling that sense of familiarity that comes from being home at the same time as apprehending the tug of the unfamiliar, of a kingdom that is to come. A church that gestures between past, present and future *in its very essence*. A church that dwells with diversity, not containing it but enabling us to see it as an outworking of God's plan for his creation.

The Church of England is a gift to the nation: a light that burns, perhaps dimly but persistently, for the whole neighbourhood, asking for nothing in return. It is a part of our very fabric: a national church present locally, reminding us that we all belong somewhere, even when we find ourselves anywhere and everywhere. These are the characteristics that we need to preserve, to cherish and celebrate. Because if we keep the faith, if we maintain our "grammar of obedience", we'll rediscover our bearings and find our way back home.

"The Little Boy Lost" suggests a further paradox on top of the many I have put forward in this essay. The Church of England, it seems to me, is both the little boy in the mire, always at risk of losing its way, and the vapour itself. For many, it is the means by which life is navigated, even when they are out in the mire—or perhaps especially at that moment. For we know, don't we, that the church is reached for with greater urgency in times of hardship, when we feel lost as a nation. After mass shootings or terrorist attacks, in times of national and global emergency such as the COVID-19 pandemic of 2020-1. When, locally or individually, we experience illness or bereavement. That's when we look for the light of the church, finding it reassuring even if we are unable to step closer to it because of the pain in our hearts. The light still burns, the vapour glows and we are grateful for those who keep it aflame.

Of course, we are only the *pro tem* keepers of the light, as the second poem in Blake's sequence makes plain. For in "The Little Boy Found", we are reminded that, wherever we wander, the Father comes to us, bathed in glory and calling us home:

> The little boy lost in the lonely fen,
> Led by the wandering light,
> Began to cry, but God, ever nigh,
> Appeared like his father in white.

This speaks of something important in our journeying, simultaneously letting us off the hook and calling us to an ever-closing keeping of the discipline of humility that is part of following Christ. Whatever we do, God is ever nigh, even when we lose our bearings. Unlike the narrative of the sports hall, in which we maintain God's presence through our faithfulness, in this understanding it is God's presence that *prompts* our faithfulness. Or, to put that differently, it is because God is faithful that we are faithful, as Paul remarks in that discourse in Romans 9 about election, as I tried to explore in my faltering words from the pulpit of Westminster Abbey. The meaning of covenant is that God is with us, "ever nigh". All we need are eyes to see him.

The subject and object in worship

One way to characterize this is through a distinction between the object and the subject in worship. We, the worshippers, are subjects, while God, the worshipped, is the object. That means worship is more about God than it is about us. It is something he asks of us, as the Hebrew Bible and the New Testament make plain, not because he needs to bask in our glorification but because disciplined worship of the Father in heaven, through the Son and the Holy Spirit, is the means by which we are formed for the kingdom. It is, as I have been arguing, the gesturing between memory and becoming that foretastes God's promise and puts us in the way of his presence.

If we foreground the subject—ourselves—in worship, we miss the point. More importantly, we leave the light behind, bathed as we are in a glow of our own making: the reinforcement of our taste or fancy, of what makes us feel good. There is a discipline to liturgy, to all prayer. Sometimes it comes easily, but most of the time it is difficult. I trudge to my study at dawn most days, pausing in my journey through the kitchen only to make a cup of tea, and start my day with the morning office. Some days I'd sooner spend the time looking at pictures of Land Rovers on the internet or shopping for books. On those occasions, I force myself to pray. It is the discipline that forms you.

The same is true of our worship in church, of which our personal keeping of the hours is a form of dedicated participation. It is not that what I do in my study is for me and what I do in church is for the community. It is all a part of the church's worship, joining with the communion of the saints and putting ourselves, and the lives of all those whose presence we represent through our faithful keeping of God's time, in the way of God's grace, in the light of his kingdom. When we worship, we foreground the object, God. That is our discipline. Incidentally, that is why in the catholic tradition priests wear chasubles. They are not—or shouldn't be—about dressing up in fancy attire. They are about foregrounding the object such that the priest at the altar is no longer this or that person we see in the village pub or out with her dogs on a morning but a representation of God, present in Christ, with us in our thanksgiving and praise.

Two things are at work in worship when it is construed as subjects putting themselves in the way of God rather than as a subjective experience the success of which can be measured by *how we feel*. First, we are made as a community that is fit for purpose. As St Paul wrote to the Christians at Corinth (giving the lie to the notion that the abandonment of liturgy would somehow herald a return to the simplicity of the early church):

> The cup of blessing that we bless, is it not a sharing in the blood of Christ? The bread that we break, is it not a sharing in the body of Christ? Because there is one bread, we who are many are one body, for we all partake of the one bread.
> *1 Corinthians 10:16–17*

It is through our disciplined keeping of God's company in worship that we are formed as the kind of community I have been describing: one of paradox and tension, in which difference is celebrated as the means by which we express our longing for the kingdom and which does not divide us. If worship is reduced to subjectivism, to how *I feel in this moment*, it will not hold us together, even though our shared elation at being saved may seem to give us far more in common than the language of "common prayer". The unity is illusory because it is grounded in our preferences rather than that which goes beyond us and all the time calls us home.

Second, worship in which God is foregrounded is worship in which our dispositions are shaped, our desires educated, to see the world as God sees it. As the scholar Laurence Paul Hemming writes, drawing on St Thomas Aquinas: "Redemption will mean that our minds will be perfected, and we will be able to see *as* God sees and see *what* God sees (in so far as God chooses)."[30] Hemming's wider thesis is that (liturgical) worship is the means by which we foretaste redemption, configuring ourselves for the glory of God's kingdom. What we glimpse in those rare moments of becoming that happen infrequently in our worship is that experience of seeing as God sees and seeing what God sees. It stands to reason that the more we worship in this way, the more we are trained for such seeing (and the more subjective our worship, the less likely we are to apprehend the world as the object of worship sees it). This circles back to my previous point: if we abandon worship that is difficult, because it is not principally to do with *our* feelings but with expressing our faithful longing for God, we may step further away from God. We may lose our bearings.

This has a lot to do with glory since it is glory that we apprehend fleetingly in our worship. Inevitably, our knowledge of glory both shapes and is shaped by our understanding and experience of worship. If we understand God's glory to be manifested in miraculous healings or a sense that every facet of our lives is open to his intervention, we will configure worship to conjure such a God. If we understand glory as something more universal, nonetheless revealed in the particularity of our worship in a given place at a given time as a given people, then we configure worship that is centred on the object and worries not about efficacy since it understands that the kingdom does not permit measurement, that the most we can say about it is of its abundance, which is always beyond compare.

So we need to ask what sort of glory we long for as a community. That telescope that we have been turning around and around throughout this essay—it needs to be pointed in the right direction. If not, we could make God seem very small, even as we try to make him bigger. The point, I suppose, is that God is at *both ends*: in among the minutiae of our lives through the incarnation and, through that same act, calling us to something that transcends the detail, that takes us beyond ourselves. The effects of worship cannot be measured, therefore, either in numbers attending or in prayers answered. Because it is our disciplines of corporate prayer (our "grammar of obedience"), with God in the foreground, that make us ready for the kingdom and give us eyes to see it. It is precisely when we are taken out of ourselves and see the world as God sees it that we perceive glory. That such glory cannot be measured is of course a challenge for those of us who want to see our beloved Church of England flourish. But of one thing we can be sure: if we abandon our essence in the pursuit of numerical growth, we will find that we are further from home than ever.

While it is some comfort to know that God will find us, no matter what, dressed in white and leading us by the hand, we should want more for ourselves and for God. Glory is growth into God's kingdom, not growth for its own sake. We strive not to wander away from the vapour but to keep its flame aglow. In faithfulness, we keep God's company, we keep God's time and the whole earth receives a glory that cannot be numbered.

CHAPTER 7

Marking time

St Mary's, Isle Abbots

The Church of St Mary is reckoned to be one of the most beautiful in Somerset. It is our home now, where my children were baptized, where I celebrated my first mass as a priest. It is the church I went to as soon as I could after life-changing surgery, knowing it would bring solace, that it would help make me feel whole again. Oddly, it is not in the village where we live but across the road, deeper into the countryside. But it is home, nonetheless. Something about it resonated with me when I first visited years ago to lead a quiet service of evening prayer. The people then were welcoming but rather suspicious: who was this black-robed character stepping into their midst? Over the years, we grew together, forming an intimacy that binds us in our particularity, helping us apprehend our transcendence in each other's company.

Today is Plough Sunday, the first Sunday after Epiphany. There is an ancient, now unused, plough in the church, along with milk churns and hay, seed from last year's harvest (I was there when the combine plucked it from the field, my son in the cab alongside the farmer) and soil (orange, of course). We have a service sheet that involves participation from the local farmers, who stand reverently and speak their lines with sincerity and purpose. I am struck, as always, by the quality of light in this ancient building, the way it plays on the stonework and pools at the high altar. The adornments are simple: a coloured cloth to reflect the liturgical season (white today because we are in a season of celebration until Candlemas in early February) laid over perfectly pressed linen, a modest brass collection plate, a wooden cross. There is something of unnerving beauty in this simplicity. I am moved every time I see it, even more so when I see the tenderness with which the churchwarden dresses the altar before a Eucharist. Like his father before him, he takes care to place everything so that it is just so, taking the same pride in this small act of co-creation as he does in sowing his fields and tending to his herd.

But it is the timing of our celebration that focuses my attention today. A coincidence of things temporal and things eternal, the like of which happens with pleasing regularity in the church's calendar. By tradition, tomorrow (Plough Monday) would be the first day agricultural workers went out into the fields after the Christmas break. So this service is a back-to-work blessing, a chance to express hope and longing that the labour in the fields over the coming months yields a good harvest. It is also an expression of faith in God's purposes, belief that he will provide. Or, at least, it is recognition that God is ultimately in control, even while we strive to find our place in the world by responding to his love. Finally, it is a chance for the community to give thanks to the people who work to feed them, to bless the hands that till the soil and feed the sheep. That is what I find so moving: the sense in which this community marks the work of the people in its midst, recognizing that in their labour is seen a different sort of meeting between heaven and earth.

The timing makes some kind of sense in relation to the agricultural calendar, therefore, even though the proliferation of winter wheat means that most ploughing was done long ago in the autumn. And, anyway, most farmers wouldn't dream of taking a whole two weeks off after Christmas nowadays. But the symbolism obtains. And it works especially well liturgically because, in God's time, marked as it is by the changing of the church's seasons, the feast of Epiphany is a moment in which all of our hopes are focused on recognition of the Christ child as present to the whole world, not just in the particularity of the Jewish community into which he was born. The magi represent the gentiles, those who are beyond the specific context in which Jesus's life plays out. When they visit the newborn Messiah, they serve as symbols that he is Christ for everyone, known in a specific place, at a specific time, among a specific people, but gesturing to the universal, always towards a generality.

Our gesture is similar: from the past of our context, in which the workers enjoyed a last day of leisure before returning to the fields, via the present of our gathered community today, towards the future harvest that we will give thanks for in this same church, with this same cast of characters, in late September. In so gesturing, through our liturgy that speaks of hope in God's majesty over creation and our partnership in tending the land and helping it bear fruit, we reach back to Eden, into our present relationship with God as those who have glimpsed his kingdom and yearn for its coming and towards that time when God will be all in all, and we shall see as God does and be made whole.

Our worship in time takes us out of time. It is precisely because of the specificity of this event, with these people, that we are able to apprehend that which goes beyond us but always calls us home. It is how we keep our bearings, preventing the vapour from flying away. In worship, we are thrown ever deeper into our particularity, knowing that it is all we have as a means of expressing our shared longing for our future. This Plough Sunday service is located precisely at the intersection of time and eternity. I think this as I experience the specificity of the cool metal of the plough blades against my fingertips or the dryness of the stored wheat grain in my outstretched palms. As I hold clods of orange soil that represent this landscape that I love, that is the backdrop of our life together as a community in this place, I realize that this is what it means to be home, amid all that is familiar, knowing that it will all be transcended, that it has already become the past as I finish the final hymn and blessing and make my way out to the back door to say my farewells. Already it has passed to unfamiliarity, to something I once knew and through which I was known. And yet it lingers because it will always be my heart, still beating, with these people in this place.

My friends in Isle Abbots are used to my damp eyes when I stand at the back of church after a service. It's a regular occurrence. But they understand why this particular service has affected me so much. It is the language of hope that is hardwired into our blessings and thanksgivings on Plough Sunday that strikes a chord. The liturgy recognizes that, in our striving, we acknowledge God's bounteous grace, living faithfully in the light of his promises to us and trusting in his future, while at the same time knowing that we play our part, that we must keep the faith and configure our longing towards his kingdom. They notice how, unconsciously, I touch my side as I speak about trust in the future. They detect the slight falter in my voice that betrays my frailty. They know that I'm still not confident in my earthly future, even while I stand with them to face heaven. They know me, deeply and profoundly, such that our intimacy as a community goes beyond words. At that moment, in that shared hope that makes sense of all our individual hopes, large and small, we glimpse God's glory that both is and is to come. We gesture, together, in our time, knowing that in doing so we stand a chance of putting ourselves in God's time, however fleetingly. On Plough Sunday, we keep God's time because we mark it by reference to our time. In worship, we offer to God what is going on in our communities, and in our lives, and set it all in the light of his promises to us. And so we apprehend his glory and glimpse what it will be to see the world as he does, to see what he does.

Marking time

> There is no cessation to the passage of time. There are good days and bad ones, times of plenty and times of desperation, seasons of agony and seasons of delight. Eventually, we presume, the weaver runs out of thread, a sign that things are coming to an end. But in the meantime, the passage of time is relentless. It cannot be made to go more slowly. It will not pass any faster than it already does. It is impossible to tame it. Our only hope is to mark it, sanctify it, relax into it, enjoy it, and allow life to be shaped by the inevitability of its passage.[31]

So begins a handbook to liturgical timekeeping, capturing the odd tension at work in our Christian worship, which the Plough Sunday service evinces with particular economy. I keep this quotation pasted above my desk. It helps me maintain perspective and is especially motivating on mornings when observance of the hours feels unwelcome or strange, when I'd sooner be ogling cars on the internet or searching for my next thriller. For the truth of the matter is that we cannot control time. We cannot tame it. But we can mark it and in doing so seek to glimpse its transcendence, reaching beyond our experience of one thing after another to see something of the time beyond time which only God curates.

That is what happens in liturgy. It is what the liturgical seasons are all about: marking human time in recognition that it's only a part of our story, our means of glimpsing eternity. You could say that there is a distinction between perceived time (human) and real time, which is God's time. Perceived time is hours, minutes, seconds, ticking away regardless of how we live, what we do, who we become. Real time is God's time; it is the rhythm of our lives that we feel in our deep heart's core. It is what we are as much as how we live. It is found in the moment at which our lives, our individual stories and those of our community, find their place in God's story. And then they make sense.

I can't help returning to Leo in *The Wanderers* as the swans fly overhead. It seems to me that his sense of time somehow collapsing into itself as the birds recede to the future is exactly what liturgical timekeeping is all about. That is why worship often makes us feel uneasy: we see the shape of something rising ahead but can't recognize it until it passes. Perhaps the shapes that we glimpse in worship are ourselves, unfathomable even to ourselves but made startlingly clear as we recede into our own future. Perhaps the shape is also God, calling us to his kingdom, known fleetingly and for all time in Christ, who joins us on the ridge and understands what it is to live amid our human mess and muddle, in the very midst of our unknowing.

These experiences tell us that liturgy has something important to do with time. When we disconnect the two, we impoverish our worship because we take ourselves out of the very contexts in which we may find ourselves able to enter God's time. We need to be located *here and now* in order to see that which goes beyond us. Lose the here and now, and you lose the beyond-ness that it somehow contains.

Flick through *Common Worship*, and you'll see that it's all about setting human time into the context of God's life in Christ. As Bishop Robert Atwell writes in his lucid handbook to worship: "Beginning afresh on Advent Sunday, the liturgical year is constructed around seasons and observances. It sets time against eternity. It celebrates an understanding of the world as the theatre of God's grace and sees human beings as created beings searching for meaning and purpose in response to his call."[32] That is the very essence of the liturgical calendar: not a pick-and-mix set of possibilities but a disciplined observance of the rhythms of prayer and thanksgiving through which we mark our passage through life and set ourselves in the way of God's eternal promises. It is precisely through shared recognition that we are beings *in time* that we are capable of locating ourselves through prayer and worship at the meeting point of time and eternity.

Seasonality is the essence of worship. Separate our praise of God from our being in time, and you make just as big a mistake as you do when failing to recognize the importance of place. Anywhereville becomes Anytimeville, reading whichever Gospel the preacher feels they have something to talk about that day, praying whatever prayers come in the moment, without asking if they *mean* anything, if they make any difference to our being and becoming. You close down the gesture, limit it, locating it only in the particular rather than the general. The subject dominates the object, and the object disappears from view.

Mark time *faithfully*, however, and you'll see the intimate connection between context and our knowing of God. Even the liturgical colours reinforce our sense of who we are at any given moment: green for those chunks of ordinary time in spring and summer when the fields and trees are bursting with life; purple in the drear days of autumn and winter, when our hearts are heavy and our energy low; red when we are aflame with hope as Christ enters Jerusalem, at Whitsun and in the crisp golden days of November; and white or gold when we are suffused with joy amid the sparkling light of Christmas or the sheer joy at new life of Eastertide. Liturgical time makes sense of our time, not just on occasions like Plough Sunday when the church and world are joined in hope but in other seasons, when there is a coincidence of mood between society and the faithful keeping of God's time.

Consider Remembrance Sunday as a case in point. It falls in the Kingdom Season, a time in which we look with hope and certainty towards the glory that is to come and remember those who have already been called to it, who have receded into the future. It is a month in which we focus upon what we are configured to see in every act of worship, just as we do in our Sunday-by-Sunday observance of Easter: hope and glory. The liturgical seasons always work in this way: drawing out a rhythm and instilling in us a *habitus* that is a feature of the Christian way of life. Think, for example, of the collect that is prayed every Friday evening in *Common Worship* Night Prayer:

> Lord Jesus Christ, Son of the Living God,
> who at this evening hour lay in the tomb
> and so hallowed the grave
> to be a bed of hope for all who put their trust in you:
> give us such sorrow for our sins,
> which were the cause of your passion,
> that when our bodies lie in the dust,
> our souls may live with you forever. Amen.[33]

It can be hard to make it through that prayer without weeping. It is a weekly reminder of the cost of the cross, of the horror of Christ's crucifixion and the hope it nonetheless contains. It sets each weekend up as an observance of the Triduum, an apprehension of the deep sorrow of Good Friday, the pain of Holy Saturday and the profound joy of Easter, and therefore of the whole pattern of Christian living. Thus it reminds us of the incomparable love that is at the heart of our relationship with God: we are the cause of his passion, and yet he draws us always into his heart, into his kingdom, promising to make us whole, hallowing the grave.

That is what we mark on Remembrance Day, gathered around our community's representation of the hallowed graves of the fallen. We see the particularity of grief written on the faces of our neighbours: the mothers who lost sons in Iraq and Afghanistan; the children, now in their old age, whose fathers never returned from Normandy; the men whose brothers were killed on manoeuvres, not even fighting in a war. And we see more loss besides: the loss that is marked in this season of remembrance through All Souls' Day. The grief felt at every passing, somehow signalled in the red and occasional white of the poppies, the sombre words taken from John Maxwell Edmonds: "For our tomorrow, they gave their today." Yes, that is the rub: this is about today and tomorrow, suspending our now in the thwarted future of those who have gone too soon, understanding that our grief is located in a missing past.

So, you see, the church's seasons aren't just for the holy few who gather faithfully week by week. Observing them keeps *us all* holy in our communities. It is why the inhabitants of the nation look to the parish church in their midst, representative as it is of both the general and the particular, in time and out of time, that which is at once familiar and unfamiliar. We all understand, at some intuitive level, that our very being in time is made sense of in a unique way through the disciplined curation of time, its marking, that is the very essence of the parish church.

To understand why, it is helpful to return to the past, even as we apprehend the future. To go back to the ridge and watch the shapes of tomorrow and yesterday rising ahead of us and behind us, uncertain as we are of their form. To think again of Romans 9 and the continuity between God's call to Abraham and his call to us. To go back to Eden and remember what we are made for. To dwell amid the sorrowful time of Good Friday even as it reaches towards Easter, Ascensiontide and the glory that is to come. Each of these experiences of our imagination remind us of the truth that Sam Wells expresses when he writes, following Karl Barth: "God's original choice [is] never to be except to be for us in Christ . . . To be God's companions: that is the nature and destiny of humankind."[34]

The parish church is the place in which God's choice for creation is made real, Sunday by Sunday, week by week, month by month. As the seasons pass, as the cloth on the altar at St Mary's changes colour along with the rhythms of village life—the ploughed fields, the harvested grain, the disruptions of illness and bereavement, the falling leaves that spring to life again—we hold out to the world the promise that God has chosen to be for us in the particularity of our lives, of our place and time, always holding up for us our destiny: that we shall be transcended and made glorious.

That is what we preserve and curate, with care, when, faithfully, we keep God's time: recognition for ourselves and for our whole community that we are God's companions, that we are never alone. Sometimes, on Remembrance Day or at Christmas or Easter, or on days like Plough Sunday if you're in the deep countryside, the whole community joins in our timekeeping, turning its eyes from the present to the past and the future in one shared gesture. For the most part, we do it on their behalf, cupping our hands around the light of hope and knowing that, if only we keep the faith, the whole world will be suffused with that light.

Understanding that, it is easy enough to consider the final piece of this jigsaw I have been constructing: the question of what it is to belong to this church. We have only to carry the flame into the world, and our work will begin.

CHAPTER 8

Keeping and sharing

The Isle Valley Benefice, Somerset

It is not every day that you drive with an orange balanced in your cup holder, still less one with a candle poking out of the centre and four cocktail sticks loaded with gummy sweets and raisins around the edge. At least I have blown out the flame, though I fully intend to light it again once I stop. I am making what seems like the most precious delivery of the day: a Christingle at the start of Advent, signalling our hope in Christ the light of the world and our thanksgiving for his bounteous goodness. There is a red stripe made of ribbon around the middle, symbolizing the blood of Christ's sacrifice on the cross. But it is the candle that dominates. It is always the light.

The recipient didn't know he had an interest in this light until a week or so ago. His existence seemed permanently dark and getting darker. The cancer was spreading, with no hope of a cure. A scientist by training, he was suspicious of that which cannot be proved and so had dismissed faith as intellectually untenable. Yet here he was, facing his ending and asking to see a priest.

When I walked into his room, it was as if two souls that were always destined to form a friendship had finally been brought together. Within moments we discovered one another's love of Rachmaninov, spoke about poetry, enjoyed a consideration of the uncertainty and perplexity of quantum mechanics. We didn't talk about the light, though we knew its flame was kindling, even as he explained his reasons for dismissing the possibility of its glow.

Over the course of a week or so, my regular visits were a moment of mutual becoming. We didn't pray together for some time but slowly edged our way towards an understanding. I wasn't there to make a conversion. He wasn't ready to abandon a viewpoint founded on a lifetime's intelligent consideration. Death does strange things but rarely overcomes the force of an intellect like his. Our understanding was this: I would create the space in which his unbelief could be held in tension with my belief. The two would come together to form not a middle ground but a shared space in which we could dwell together. Eventually, prayer felt an acceptable part of our routine, just a psalm or a reading from the mystics. If *The Wanderers* had been written by then, I'd have certainly read the passage about Leo and the swans. We both knew the terms in which prayer was uttered: it spoke to the space between us, where our knowing and unknowing could take flight.

So now I am here with a small token of what happens when you focus your attention on that space, when you give it your all. The Christingles were blessed moments ago, in an unruly service aimed mainly at children. We sang songs. We ate biscuits and drank squash. We laughed and sometimes shrieked as we shared excitement at the thought of Christmas. And then we were still, gathered around the just-sparked flame as it multiplied and filled the church, passing from candle to candle in the cool evening air. Together, we knew that it was a flame we needed to share to spread the light. And so we went, resolving to take our oranges around the village and share the light we had been keeping aflame.

Which is why I find myself hunkered beside the hedge outside the house and trying to fire my lighter. It can be harder to keep a flame alive once you take it outside of church, outside of its protection. The world has many crosswinds. But, cupping my hands so closely around it that I can feel the heat gently singeing my palms, I make it to the porch, pressing my nose against the bell so as not to leave the light exposed. That will come later.

Inside, the candle burns taller, as if the angels are with me, keeping it alight. But I notice my friend's focus is only momentarily on the flame. He fingers the blood-red ribbon around the orange, suddenly aware of an ending in which his own makes sense: an ending that isn't an ending because it is shot through with hope.

The hope comes from the sheer materiality of Christ's death. Blood and gore, pain and sorrow. These are the words by which we understand the crucifixion. They are human words, signalling a suffering that is all too real. But above, as on the Christingle, always hangs the hope of redemption, that death will be overcome, that the light will shine. In church, we never see the cross without also seeing the resurrection in the candles on the altar or scattered around the building. Darkness is always juxtaposed with light. Suffering with joy. Time with eternity. Apart from on Good Friday, when the church is blank, no candles alight, the church always reminds us of the transitive quality of suffering. The Christingle that a dying man holds now in his hands is that in microcosm: blood and light, the fallen world and its glorification. Small wonder that he focuses on the ribbon. It is the pain that makes the light burn brighter still.

As per our tacit agreement, this is no conversion. We know what he doesn't believe. But it is a moment of grace for both of us. Eyes shining in the gloom of his cottage, we know that something has passed between us, that our lives have changed for the better. For me, it is a sense of having apprehended the transcendent. For him, it is perhaps that he has been given hope, albeit a hope that he finds unintelligible. But that doesn't matter. I can hold it on his behalf. All he needs to see is the flame.

Sometimes that flame burns brightly of its own accord. I think of my friends Robin and Delia from another village down the road. For the last year or so, their parish church has been closed for repair. Like many rural churches, it was falling down, unsafe to enter. But as so often happens in these circumstances, the community rallied, raising the money needed to save it. Now it is shrouded in scaffold and bright-white boarding, a church on Holy Saturday: its glory obscured while it is remade.

But actually, the glory (or, rather, our apprehension of it) has just moved, down the road, to Robin and Delia's house. They have hosted a regular Eucharist, turning their living room into a holy space, with altar set beside the window and chairs arranged in a semi-circle on either side. Step into the room and you instantly realize you are on holy ground. It is peaceful and calm but more than that: it is a place in which everything is open, where no possibilities are closed down. It has become the church for this community because it is a place that was available for sanctification, ready to receive the light. The stillness is tangible. We all notice it when a service ends. It's as if we are frightened to break into it, to interrupt the silence with our thoughts of coffee and homemade biscuits. But of course the glory continues because this is a place in which prayer is valid, where we are known fully and wait to be known. It is a place where heaven meets earth.

I am not surprised when Delia tells me one day that she lights a candle in that room at the same time every day as she says her evening prayers. You can feel that flame every time you enter, sense its glow and feel its warmth. She has been cupping her hands around that flame for years, in church and in her home. Keeping it alight and sharing it with the world.

Keeping and sharing. That is all we are called to do. Whether it is taking a Christingle to the house of a dying man or lighting the flame each day, faithfully, and bringing the concerns of the community before God, praying that it may bask in his light. We keep the faith. And then, in our own modest ways, when the moment requires, we share it.

It is the keeping that matters. For, if Delia didn't light her candle every day, what would she have to share?

A fortunate calling

The Dominican theologian Timothy Radcliffe writes beautifully about the life of discipleship and the way that worship trains us for the kingdom. In one of his books, *Why Go to Church?* (2008), he answers the question posed in the title with elegant simplicity: "Why go to church? To be sent from it."[35]

Radcliffe's comment is a helpful corrective at the end of this narrative. It helps us remember to avoid "churchiness". It reminds us that we are called to live our faith in the world, not in the midst of the church building with all its beauty, with all its holiness. That is simply where we go for its renewal, to dwell in the midst of God's glory and glimpse his kingdom. But in being called to that place, to that worship, we are also being sent into the world to share the light that we keep burning, even in modest ways, to show the world that there is a hope like no other, in which suffering and pain are overcome, in which joy is unconfined.

There is a twofold implication to this: first, we need to look after the flame, to nurture it and protect it. Let's avoid anything that risks extinguishing it. Even if only four of us, and perhaps a dog, gather around it, we're keeping it burning for the whole world. Count the people and you count the wrong thing. Just think of the light, spreading even as we cup our hands and keep it burning. As one of the Desert Fathers observed: "If you will, you can become all flame." Second, we need to understand what it is we're sharing and seek to do it faithfully and with integrity.

I've never been a great one for making conversions. I'm a failed priest in that regard. But I will gladly carry the light of Christ's hope into the world, showing how faith in it makes a difference to us all, embodying hope in the redemption that is our weekly re-enactment in the liturgy. And I make no bones: what I do in church I do for the community, holding its particularity before God in sure and certain hope that, in doing so, something of God's glory will be made known in this place. As a priest, I see myself as holding a community of representation: what we do we do on behalf of you all. Keep the faith, then share it through our living witness.

It has always been my view that communities need this hope in glory at their very centre. As I have said already, they reach for it in times of duress, in times of joy and celebration. There are moments—perhaps when their parish church is threatened with closure, or when a royal couple are married, or when individual, community or national disaster strikes—when they turn their eyes to the church, expecting its light to be burning brightly in their midst. They rely on us faithfully to bring them before God and show that there is always the possibility of being transcended, of being configured towards a glory that is known but not yet fully known.

To make this point, I inevitably think about the role of the priest because that's what I am: it is my vocation in the *oikonomia* of the church. But what I say about the priest I mean for all believers, since what is a priest if not the one called to represent, and model, the life of discipleship to which we are all called? While there are differences in our way of serving, largely understood by reference to our role in the celebration of the sacraments, there is a sense that, when it comes to living the faith, what obtains for the priest obtains for all believers. If there is a pattern of discipleship, it is found as much in my life as in that of my fellow Christians. We are in this together.

In order to think more of priests, I want to think first of a country doctor. This one in particular is the focus of John Berger's stunning book, *A Fortunate Man* (1967), which tells us much about the longings of a community and how they are configured. Berger writes the story of John Sassall, a GP in the Forest of Dean. As he sets out his understanding of Dr Sassall's role in the communities he serves, it is perhaps inevitable that Berger should draw a comparison with the parish priest. Both roles, after all, are regarded as professional but deeply embedded in the community. Both are somehow set apart at the same time as being drawn ever deeper into the specific mores of a given place and time. And both, in their own ways, are concerned with healing.

In a telling reflection, Berger concentrates on the perceived "otherness" of Sassall, saying that he represents something that goes beyond the community in which he lives and works. He notes Sassall's separation from the people he serves on the basis of education but also because he hears their secrets, helps narrate their lives. Sassall, you might say, is an "anywhere" person, thrown into a community of "somewhere", a neighbourhood. He has a particular role to play, helping them make sense of their lives, helping them feel fully known. Thus, Berger:

> Some may now assume that [Sassall] has taken over the role of the parish priest or vicar. Yet this is not so. *He is not the representative of an all-knowing, all-powerful being. He is their own representative.* His records will never be offered to any higher judge. He keeps records so that, from time to time, they [the residents of his village] can consult them themselves. The most frequent opening to a conversation with him, if it is not a professional consultation, are the words 'Do you remember when ... ?' *He represents them, becomes their objective (as opposed to subjective) memory, because he represents their lost possibility of understanding, and relating to the outside world, and because he also represents some of what they know but cannot think.*[36]

There is much to dwell on here. It is a microcosm of Berger's book as a whole, perhaps of his whole life's work. He is concerned with the movement from the particular to the universal and back again. He captures something of a life we all know, regardless of our context, by engaging in detailed critical analysis of the particularity of a community in the Forest of Dean: of, *in particular*, the life of their doctor.

There is a clear continuity between Berger's methodological assumptions and mine in as much as he believes in the power of the particular to explicate the general and vice versa. But remember, Berger is a Marxist and existentialist: he assumes that there is no transcendent other, that this world is *all there is*. Small wonder, then, that, for Berger, Sassall constitutes the "objective" presence in the community: a scientific expert, someone who brings objectivity by reference to a discourse of fact rather than faith. His implication is that the doctor brings "truth" to the community and its people, which for Berger loosely relates to self-actuation or "recognition"—a psychological word meaning "being known".

The priest, meanwhile, offers something different. That's why Berger is at pains to show the difference between the two roles in a community. We could characterize it thus: the doctor is this-worldly; the objectivity they bring is material, grounded in what we know. The priest, meanwhile (and I would want to say all Christian disciples called to share God's love and justice), is of another kingdom but nonetheless, like Christ, thrown into the milieu of temporality and geography. Their objectivity is spiritual; it comes from a higher authority. What they bring may well be "recognition", but it is a deeper, more profound sense of being known, fully, even in our becoming. It is that knowing that I encounter in the walls of Christ Church, Fairwarp, in that church in Geneva, in St Peter's, Ilton and St Mary's, Isle Abbots—in all the churches I have been describing. A knowing that understands there is yet more to come in the glorious kingdom of God.

So there is a fundamental difference between the rural GP and the priest. We can capture it by comparing Berger's description of the doctor to Archbishop Michael Ramsey's description of the priest in his seminal *The Christian Priest Today* (1972):

> The priest *displays* in his (sic!) own person that total response to Christ to which all members of the Church are pledged. He is to be a "beacon" of the Church's pastoral, prophetic and priestly concern. "By ordination a Christian becomes a sign of the ministry of Jesus Christ in his Church" [a quotation from Max Thurian's *Studia Liturgica*]. Besides displaying the Church's response the priest also *enables* it, for by his professional training and concentration of labour he "gets things done". And besides displaying and enabling he also *involves* the whole Church in his own activity. When he visits a sick person, for instance, it is not only

> the visit of a kind Christian; it is the Church visiting. Similarly the priest can be the Church praying, the Church caring for the distressed, the Church preaching. In the Church and for the Church he *displays,* he *enables,* he *involves.*[37]

Ramsey's comments are certainly of their time, hence the lack of gender-inclusive language and the innate clericalism. But with some interpretation, we see the difference the priest, the holy person, the public Christian (which is all of us whose lives are configured by our shared worship of God in the parish church), makes to the community. They are a beacon of hope, a beacon of otherness. They show every community, and the whole nation, what it is to be transcended, to understand that this world isn't all there is, that there is a light that burns for us all.

So it is that we discern our dual call: keep the faith and share the faith. Keep it in our liturgies, in our gestures of memory and becoming. Keep the parish church, and thus the community it represents, as the meeting place of time and eternity, of earth and heaven. Even if we are few in number, model what it is to live with difference, to love in spite of disagreement and conflict. Hold the space in between. Mark time, measure the changing of the seasons, enter into the particularity of each person's life. Be God's presence in the neighbourhood. Then share the glimpses of his glory in the community where you are present. Make it home. Carry the flame of the Christingle, casting its dim light on the blood of the cross, into the communities you are called to love and serve. Keep the flame burning in your living room, in your private prayer. Bring hope to the dying, love to the unloved, healing to the wounded, wholeness to the broken.

Do these things because you can think of doing nothing else. Expect nothing in return. Just keep the faith and share the faith. Then the whole world will know what it is to be loved.

CODA

The parish in lockdown

Zoom Church, the internet

The screen before me is temporarily blank. I have forgotten my password. But then, finally, I am allowed access, and a sea of fifty-five faces awaits. They are of the people I love, my friends in this neighbourhood of becoming in which I respond most fully to my priestly call. A few months ago, we would never have dreamt of meeting for worship in this way. Even Delia's living room felt like a stretch for some. But dialling into a video conference, to "Zoom Church" as we have come to call it, would have been anathema. Something for other denominations to try: those that have a looser understanding of place, let alone the importance of formal liturgy.

And yet the parish church is now online. Not just this parish but *all* parishes, *everywhere*. It is borne of necessity since our churches have been closed, on and off, all year and even now are open only for private prayer. A pandemic has swept the world, forcing every community into lockdown. For whole chunks of time many of the most vulnerable are advised not to leave home, even for a walk. The rest are allowed one excursion a day. And, for the most part, the doors of the parish church have been locked shut. The risk of infection is too high.

So we moved it all online. And now we gather, at least once a week, to sing and pray and break open God's word. It is a moving witness: nothing like regular church, with little in the way of liturgy, because the technology does not allow for uncluttered responses. It is, though, a powerful sign that our faith will not be tamed. That the candle burns brightly, even when the world is dark.

It is too early to reflect on the long-term impact of this crisis for our churches or for society at large. Many in religious circles began by celebrating a renewal. According to a study, one in four adults accessed some kind of religious ceremony online during the various lockdowns. At a local level, the thought of gathering fifty-five people in one building every Sunday for weeks on end would be the stuff of a parish priest's dreams. So perhaps there is a revival, of sorts, though I doubt the numbers will stick. That's the point about religion: for many it is there when needed, waiting. It is for others to keep it alive in the meantime.

This crisis, then, bears out the essence and form of the Church of England as I have been imagining it in different ways throughout this essay. We are there when needed, but that doesn't mean we are not valued in the times in between. It is our very faithfulness that makes us loved. That evensong in St Peter's, when the world was different and village cricketers could hug in celebration on the green: it matters because it is a living embodiment of that faithfulness I have been describing. Four people cupping their hands around a flame, keeping it alight, finding evermore creative ways to bear witness to a hope that is hardwired into every community and just occasionally bubbles to the surface, even (or perhaps especially) when things look bleak.

I am sure I'm not the only one simultaneously relieved to see a proliferation of online church during the COVID crisis and rather perturbed by it. I can't bring myself to see it as an equivalent to the worship we share in church. It is perhaps best characterized as an expression of discipleship: mission growing from worship rather than worship itself. In this view, what happens when we meet online, or when my tech-savvy clergy friends post videos on social media of themselves leading services for imaginary congregations, is twofold: it is a facsimile of the worship that is at the heart of a parish, observed faithfully week by week on behalf of the community, on behalf of the whole nation; and it is a reminder that the church is here, ready to serve, bringing hope to the hopeless, light to the darkness. In other words, Zoom Church is an outworking of mission. It is best understood as what we do as a result of our worship, not the worship itself.

To think otherwise is to misjudge the nature of worship since the computer cuts through particularity and collapses easily into generality. I can just as easily worship in Geneva as I can in Ilton or Fairwarp when all

I need is a video call passcode. So what is to distinguish one online church from any other? The answer is the community that gathers, still in a given place, to pray for neighbours and friends *in that place more than any other*. The community may have moved online, but it continues to represent a *somewhere*.

Both for those who dial in and those who know only vaguely of what we do, these worshipping encounters are a visible reminder that there is a community which remains faithful, committed to a story of hope and wholeness, of love and light. They are a means of staying connected to the story, of firing our imaginations until we can meet again properly and be shaped by God's grace. And I am moved, frequently, by attending. Despite my intellectual reservations, I find this coming together of the faithful to be a profound witness. The people are particular, even if the form is universal. And, for all that, it is a public expression of hope and longing: a refusal to abandon all that we hold most dear. It is without doubt an act of the heart, constitutive of our shared growth in Christ. Maybe it's not so different from regular worship, after all.

Though what I know in my deep core is this. When the time comes, we will return to our parish churches with hearts aflame, knowing how much we have missed inhabiting these places of prayer and praise, the people, the sense of being alongside each other, of breathing the same air as we enter into God's presence, as we gesture between time and eternity. If we were told today that Zoom Church is all we have available for the rest of time, we would get on with it because that's our way. But we know that we'd give all that we have for one last evensong, for one last chance to stand with our fellow disciples, reciting canticles and psalms to the squeaks of a misbehaving pipe organ. Because that is where our hearts remain, still beating. It is where we know we are home.

We'll manage for now with the disembodied body made manifest on our screens. And when the service ends and all we are left with is a flashing cursor on the logout page and an odd feeling of both emptiness and joy, that's when we know for certain what matters most of all: that we are a faithful people, called to be Christ's presence in the midst of our communities, *no matter what*. So here now is our ending, which is also our beginning, our past and our future, mediated through the present. We keep the faith. And we make ready, always, to share it with the world.

Notes

[1] Owen Chadwick, *The Victorian Church,* Parts One and Two (London: SCM Press, 1966, 1979).

[2] Richard Dawkins, *An Appetite for Wonder: The Making of a Scientist* (London: Black Swan, 2015).

[3] Michael Ramsey, *The Gospel and the Catholic Church* (London: Longmans, Green and Co., 1936), p. 220.

[4] Michael Mayne, *The Enduring Melody* (London: Darton, Longman and Todd, 2006).

[5] Dietrich Bonhoeffer, *The Cost of Discipleship: New Edition* (London: SCM Press, 2015), first published in 1937.

[6] T. S. Eliot, *Collected Poems 1909–1962* (London: Faber and Faber, 1974), p. 201.

[7] Giovanni Maddalena, *The Philosophy of Gesture: Completing Pragmatists' Incomplete Revolution* (Montreal: McGill-Queen's University Press, 2015), especially Chapter 4.

[8] Rowan Williams, *The Edge of Words: God and the Habits of Language* (London: Bloomsbury, 2014), p. 8.

[9] Martin Heidegger, *Being and Time*, tr. John Macquarrie and Edward Robinson (Oxford: Oxford University Press, 1963).

[10] Karl Barth, *The Epistle to the Romans* (Oxford: Oxford University Press, 1933).

[11] Karl Barth, *Evangelical Theology* (Grand Rapids, MI: Eerdmans, 1963), p. 20.

[12] David Ford, *Self and Salvation: Being Transformed* (Cambridge: Cambridge University Press, 1999), pp. 171ff.

[13] Ford, *Self and Salvation*, p. 172.

[14] Ford, *Self and Salvation*, p. 176.

[15] Barth, *Romans*, p. 29.

[16] Alan Thornhill, *Three Mile Man: A Countryman's View of Nature* (Uckfield: Sweethaws Press, 1980), p. 21.

[17] Conscious of the whistle-stop character of this tour of Anglican history, I direct the interested reader to the following volume as a means of further exploration: Henry Chadwick (ed.), *Not Angels, but Anglicans: A History of Christianity in the British Isles* (Norwich: Canterbury Press, 2000).

[18] Mary Oliver, "Emerson: An Introduction", in *Upstream: Selected Essays* (New York: Penguin Press, 2016), p. 66.

[19] David Goodhart, *The Road to Somewhere: The Populist Revolt and the Future of Politics* (London: Hurst and Company, 2017), pp. 134–5.

[20] Roger Scruton, *Our Church: A Personal History of the Church of England* (London: Atlantic Books, 2012), p. 6.

[21] For more on this topic, and specifically my response to it, I invite the reader to consider Tim Gibson, "Dealing with Issues: How Does the Church of England Live with its Teaching about Homosexuality?", *Crucible: The Christian Journal of Social Ethics* (July 2013), pp. 25–32.

[22] Paul Avis, *The Anglican Understanding of the Church* (London: SPCK, 2000), p. 76.

[23] Andrew Brown and Linda Woodhead, *That Was The Church That Was: How the Church of England Lost the English People* (London: Bloomsbury, 2016), p. 154.

[24] Williams, *The Edge of Words*.

[25] Rowan Williams, "Making moral decisions", in Gill, Robin (ed.), *The Cambridge Companion to Christian Ethics* (Cambridge: Cambridge University Press, 2001), pp. 3–15, here at p. 8.

[26] Williams, "Making moral decisions", p. 9.

[27] Williams, "Making moral decisions", p. 11.

[28] Roy Strong, *A Little History of the English Country Church* (London: Vintage Books, 2007).

[29] There is a proliferation of volumes containing these collections. I have a copy that is edited by Will Jonson and published in 2013 featuring one of Blake's own engravings as the cover art.

[30] Laurence Paul Hemming, *Worship as a Revelation: The Past, Present and Future of Catholic Liturgy* (London: Burns and Oates, 2008), p. 51.

[31] J. Neil Alexander, *Celebrating Liturgical Time: Days, Weeks, and Seasons* (New York: Church Publishing, 2014), p. 1.

[32] Robert Atwell, *The Good Worship Guide* (Norwich: Canterbury Press, 2013), p. 134.

[33] The Archbishops' Council of the Church of England, *Common Worship: Daily Prayer Preliminary Edition* (London: Church House Publishing, 2002), p. 313.

[34] Samuel Wells, *God's Companions* (Oxford: Blackwell, 2006), p. 1.

[35] Timothy Radcliffe, *Why Go to Church? The Drama of the Eucharist* (London: Continuum, 2008), p. 208.

[36] John Berger, *A Fortunate Man: The Story of a Country Doctor* (London: Canongate, 1967), p. 111, my emphases.

[37] Michael Ramsey, *The Christian Priest Today* (London: SPCK, 1972, rev. edn 1985), pp. 6–7.

Lightning Source UK Ltd.
Milton Keynes UK
UKHW020803071121
393529UK00003B/9